*Acclaim for*
Never Give Up

"*In* Never Give Up, *Ruthe Rosen shares how to let go with grace and wisdom, and confirms the power of faith in facing uncertainty. Readers will find strength to accept and learn from the losses that occur in their own lives.*"
— Cynthia Wall, LCSW, author of *The Courage to Trust: a guide to building deep and lasting relationships*

"*It was an honor and a privilege to read this book. Karla was, and remains, an inspiration.* Never Give Up *will provide hope and encouragement to all who read it.*"
— Terry Maloof, associate editor,
Teacher Created Materials Publishing

"*Every mother will ache, mourn, and cry with Ruthe Rosen and be awestruck by Karla's tenacious courage.*"
— Marianne Napoles, reporter, *Chino Hills Champion*

Never Give Up

How to Find Hope and Purpose in Adversity

Karla

Ruthe Rosen

with Lisa Greathouse

Cypress House

Never Give Up
How To Find Hope and Purpose In Adversity
Copyright © 2011 by Ruthe A. Rosen

Published by Cypress House
155 Cypress Street
Fort Bragg, CA 95437
1 800 773-7782
www.cypresshouse.com

All images courtesy of the author, with the exception of the photographs on the following pages:

2: Tom Baker Photography, San Juan Capistrano, California

38: (bottom) Cheryl Schmidt

52: Pacific Imagery Professional Photography, Chino, California

70: Nikki Stuart

152: Hilde Nester

160: Photographer unknown

182: Kevin Rogers

Library of Congress Cataloging-in-Publication Data

Rosen, Ruthe, 1964-
  Never give up : how to find hope and purpose in adversity / Ruthe Rosen.
-- 1st ed.
     p. cm.
  ISBN 978-1-879384-86-6 (pbk. : alk. paper)
  1. Asch-Rosen, Karla Ann. 2. Brain--Cancer--Religious aspects--Christianity. 3. Suffering--Religious aspects--Christianity. 4. Consolation. I. Title.

BV4910.33.R67 2011
248.8'619699481--dc22

                              2011015963

PRINTED IN THE UNITED STATES OF AMERICA
1 2 3 4 5 6 7 8 9
FIRST EDITION

AMEN (a-men´)

– used to express solemn ratification (as an expression of faith) or hearty approval (as an assertion). Common English translations of the word "amen" include "verily," "truly," "so be it," and "let it be."

With love to Melinda, for your strength and courage in letting me go so I could live life to the fullest, and for giving my mom and dad the gift to choose me.

Acknowledgments

To my boys, Brandon and Cole: Thank you for continuing to keep your sister very much a part of our family. Thank you for sharing me with other kids in the foundation, and know that my love for you both remains the greatest. I promise someday it will all be worth it.

Brandon: Throughout your sister's journey you never stopped drawing her pictures, and you always made time to give her a kiss and make sure she was okay. The prayers you prayed were short, sweet, and always to the point. Karla adored you, "buddy."

Cole: So young your little heart to have so much pain. The joy of watching you and your sister cuddle in bed so often is forever in my heart. The gift of prayer she gave to you, it is my hope you will forever cherish. Karla was so proud to be your big sister, "little buddy."

To my husband Michael: You have been my strength through my pain, and for that I am forever grateful. I know that raising Karla as your stepdaughter was sometimes challenging, and it also required sacrifice on your part to allow me to have a friendship with Karla's father. From our first date until you said goodbye to Karla, you always treated her as you would your own child. But in the last four years, as we have worked together on the foundation, I have truly come to see the love and respect you have for her. Because of you, I was able to spend Karla's last year by her side, and today you still continue to allow me to give so much of my time and energy to others. Thank you for being not only my husband, but also my best friend.

To Rick: Thank you for keeping your promise of friendship while raising our daughter and for being such a great dad.

To Ginny: Thank you for allowing me to share my pain daily as I wrote and relived the journey. You always listened and encouraged me to keep writing. Thank you, Sister.

Just as going through a journey like this is too big to do alone, so is writing a book — especially when you're not a writer. I compiled Karla's journal writings and my own, the church updates that we wrote during Karla's journey, and some of the letters from others that touched my heart. Then it all sat in a binder. A year later, I began a friendship with a neighbor, Lisa Greathouse*, whom I had known for several years and whose daughter was on the dance team with Karla in junior high. When I found out Lisa was a professional writer, I asked her over for coffee. I took her up to Karla's room, sat her down in Karla's favorite chair, handed her a box of tissues and the binder, and asked her to read through it. When I came back and asked her to help me write this story, she agreed. Lisa asked another friend and neighbor, Dona Rice, who also is a professional writer and whose son was in many of Karla's classes, to help us tell Karla's story.

Lisa: You took my writings, my words, and my heart, and helped me create a book for not only me but also many others to share for years to come. For this, my friend, I will remain forever grateful.

Dona: You shared your editorial talents just as you promised, making sure that, from one mother's heart to another, you understood. For this, my friend, I will remain forever grateful.

To my friends: One day at the very beginning of Karla's journey we sat in chemo treatment and I worked on some thank-you cards. I was attempting to remember whom I needed to thank and what everyone had been giving us. I was overwhelmed. Karla looked over at me and said, "Don't even try to do that right now. You'll have the opportunity to thank everyone someday." Not fully understanding what that meant, I kept writing a few more, and then, out of frustration, I gave up. During that next year I wrote when I could, but I know there are many people Karla and I never had the chance to thank. So from the both of us:

To everyone who made a difference in our journey... you know who you are and you know what you did (and are still doing!) ... thank you from deep within my heart.

Love,
Ruthe

∼

*LISA PERLMAN GREATHOUSE, who is originally from Brooklyn, New York, worked as a journalist for The Associated Press for ten years and then for a communications/advertising agency before beginning a freelance career. She and her husband, David, and their children, Laura and Matthew, have lived in Chino Hills since 1997.

Never Give Up

Karla and me in 1990, and at my wedding in 1997

Chapter 1

There will come a time when you believe
everything is finished.
That will be the beginning.
— Louis L'Amour

EVERY MOTHER THINKS her child is special.

We all tend to zero in on the little things that make our kids seem unique, and then we magnify them, regardless of whether an objective person would ever notice. It might be a sense of humor, a keen intellect, an innate generosity, a spark they possess.

I saw all of those traits in my daughter Karla.

But if you'd met Karla when she was fourteen, she might have seemed at first glance to be a pretty typical teenage girl growing up in Southern California. She played soccer, loved to dance, enjoyed going to church, and had lots of friends. Academically, she was always at the top of her class. From the time she could read, she seemed to always have a book in her hand. I don't ever recall her coming home from elementary school with anything less than an "A," but she was the kid who always did the extra credit — just in case.

Karla loved spending time with her dad, my first husband, Rick Asch. He and I separated when Karla was four years old, and we divorced the following year. We were living in Orange County at the time, and after the split, Karla and I moved to a condo a few miles away. Rick and I promised to stay friends and always put Karla first. He stayed very involved in her life, and Karla loved seeing him and especially going with him to motocross events, where he still works on the Kawasaki Race Team. When Rick wasn't away with the team, he and Karla would often spend their time riding bicycles or trail riding on a dirt bike.

When Karla was nearly six, I met Michael Rosen, and we were married about a year later. I'll never forget dancing with Karla at our wedding to the song *Because You Loved Me*. My eyes and Karla's never left one another. Not long after, with Rick's permission, we changed Karla's name to Karla Ann Asch-Rosen as a way to help unite our new family.

In 1999, about a year after the birth of our first son, Brandon, Michael and I decided to move about thirty miles northeast to Chino Hills, a newer community where we would be able to have a bigger home for our growing family. Karla started fourth grade there, and, as the "new kid," was worried she wouldn't make friends. How wrong she was! Karla's outgoing personality seemed to always be a magnet for attention; people would often comment on her infectious smile.

A year later, in 2000, I gave birth to another son, Cole. Karla was a proud big sister, and was a huge help to me as I took care of a newborn and a toddler.

As she grew, Karla showed a passion for soccer, and Michael even coached her team for several seasons. We spent many weekends watching her travel team play, and traveled as far as Hawaii for a tournament. (Her nickname on the field was "Speedy.") Though Karla was petite at just five foot one, she was a strong athlete, and we loved watching her on the field.

When it came to her dads, Karla seemed to have the best of both worlds. When she was with Rick, there was affection, fun, and laughter. While she and Michael were close, Karla often complained that he was too strict, but she knew that she could always count on Michael to be there for every school conference and performance. Still, when Karla didn't like the way things were going at home, she could always go running to Rick… and she did.

Rick's personality is passive. Michael's personality is confident. As for me, I saw the good in both of them. However, my husband didn't always see that allowing Rick to be passive with Karla was a good thing. Though Michael was respectful of her father, at times he could be rude. Rick felt that as long as Michael was good to his daughter he didn't care what Michael thought about him. I considered Rick one of my closest friends even after my marriage to Michael. We never argued, I didn't criticize him, and I didn't try to take financial advantage of him. Before I married Michael, I told him the promise I'd made to Rick, to always be his friend, but with each passing year it got more difficult. I think in some ways Michael expected me to be inconsiderate of Rick's feelings, but I wasn't, and this was often the cause of disagreements. If it was the holidays and Rick didn't have anywhere to go, I'd say, "Why not come over to our house? That way we could both be with Karla." So without checking with Michael first, I would ask Rick. Eventually, when, out of respect for Michael's feelings, I asked for his approval, Rick always declined.

My husband reluctantly did accept my feelings, and for a while this too stood in the way of his truly embracing loving Karla the way she needed him to. Over time, a long time, we have learned to accept and respect one another's feelings.

Karla and I had a great relationship. We somehow balanced the complicated mother-daughter dynamic with being best friends. We didn't start going to church as a family until we moved to Chino Hills. But it was not until church camp as a seventh grader that Karla began to have a relationship with God. That year she and I, with our arms connected, got baptized together.

By the time Karla hit fourteen, we were both learning to navigate the turbulence of the teenage years. In eighth grade, she was on the junior high dance team and the spring-select soccer team, and was school vice president. Her grades began to slip, and she was putting time with friends above her studies. It was then that we — Michael, Rick, and I — agreed that Karla had to choose between soccer and dance. With her grades slipping as she was just about to enter high school, things could not continue at this pace. Believing that Karla would choose soccer, we told her that it was her choice and we would support her decision. So when she chose dance, let's just say I was devastated. It's not that I didn't like dance or that she didn't shine on the stage, but her talents and her passion belonged on the soccer field. Karla asked me to volunteer a few months later to be the president of the dance team, and I said yes. That decision turned out to be an unforeseen gift.

There were also the mood swings, the hormones, and every other stereotypical symptom that girls Karla's age experience.

And then there were the headaches.

I first heard about them when Karla came back from dance camp during the summer of 2004. An incoming freshman at Chino Hills High School, she had already auditioned and earned a spot on the dance team. The team had spent three days learning routines at dance camp, and Karla returned home both exhilarated and exhausted.

As she related some of the stories about camp over the next few days, she mentioned having a headache so severe that she had dropped to her knees in pain. Then came the details: She had been laughing hard just before it happened. She hadn't been wearing her glasses. She was exhausted. Her period had just started. It was easy to attribute that headache to one or any combination of those factors.

A month or two later, Karla complained again of an awful headache. When I asked, she admitted that she still wasn't wearing her glasses (she could be stubborn!). Considering how poor her eyesight was — she'd been wearing glasses since kindergarten — I was amazed she could even see without them. I pleaded with Karla to start wearing her glasses, but I also asked her to start keeping track of when her headaches occurred.

When she complained of another headache a month later, she was also showing signs of a cold, so we went to see her pediatrician. After an examination, Karla was diagnosed with a run-of-the-mill sinus infection and given a prescription for an antibiotic.

In the meantime, we'd been noticing other changes in Karla. She had always had an optimistic attitude and was most definitely a "rule follower." She'd routinely help around the house with chores and babysitting her brothers, who were then just four and seven. But now she wasn't paying attention to her grades, was constantly yelling at her brothers, and told us on more than one occasion, "You're all driving me crazy," and even, "I can't stand living with you." On top of that, she was having meltdowns in the car before dance practice, something I'd never seen from her before. She had been forgetting things, small things, like what she'd come downstairs for, homework assignments, and things we had previously told her.

Had it been any other time in her life, we probably would have been worried, but when you're a parent, it's easy to attribute things that might otherwise frighten you to whatever developmental phase your child might be going through — in this case, a teenager just entering high school. As adults, we're quick to ascribe strange behavior to "hormones"; we tend to shrug off irrational behavior and commiserate with friends who are going through seemingly similar trials with their own teens.

On Wednesday, January 5, 2005, I dropped off Karla at a friend's house, to help paint posters for a school rally that Friday. Karla was wearing her newly issued dance team jacket — you know, the one that takes eight weeks to arrive — which was part of her official team uniform. As I put the car in reverse to leave, I remember rolling down my window and calling out, "Don't forget to take your jacket off before painting." She gave me a "look" and turned to walk away. When I picked her up later and saw paint on the left shoulder of her jacket, I was furious, but what really angered me was her reaction: Instead of the remorse I expected, her response was "What's the big deal?" We argued all the way home, not only over her irresponsibility but also because of her nonchalant attitude. We were still arguing when we got home, and then Michael joined in. The more we brought up all of Karla's recent carelessness, recklessness, and irresponsibility, the more defensive she became. Never had the three of us yelled and cried so much. It was after midnight when, exhausted, we all hugged and promised to work harder to get along, and finally said goodnight.

The following morning, I awoke in a panic — we had all overslept. Karla's first class was at 6:15 a.m. and it was now 7:00, but when I ran into her room to wake her, Karla said, "Mom, my head hurts. It feels like it's going to explode."

What I wanted to say was, I'll get you some aspirin and get you to school, but I caught myself before speaking because we had just agreed to "understand" one another better.

I got Karla the aspirin and told her to go back to sleep. I called the pediatrician and made an appointment for that afternoon. As we walked into the doctor's office, Karla whispered to me, "I never took my prescription from last time, but don't tell him." Between that information and all the crying she had done the night before, the headache seemed to make sense, but Dr. Ambrose suggested an MRI; he thought the sinus infection had worsened, and he wanted a better look at her sinuses. Karla was claustrophobic, so she talked him into ordering a CT scan instead. When the doctor walked out to schedule the appointment for the following day, Karla and I calmly discussed how that was all it must be — a sinus infection that had worsened. We left with no worries, and I dropped her off at dance practice. Her first competition was in two days, on Saturday.

The next day morning, Friday, I drove Karla to school in the pouring rain. Later, I had to pull her out of school in the middle of the rally so we could make our appointment for the CT scan. My youngest, Cole, came along. It seemed like we were finished in no time and on our way home. I remember how quiet the car ride was, with only the sound of the rain outside. We stopped at a coffee shop to eat when I noticed that Karla was having trouble swallowing her food. I asked if she needed some water, and she said, "No. I've been having problems swallowing." That was the first time I remember actually being worried. She was fine for the rest of the meal, but I couldn't take my eyes off how she was eating — and I lost my own appetite.

On our way back to school for Karla's dance practice, we decided to stop at the salon near our house so she could get her nails done before the competition the next day. We were about a mile away when my cell phone rang. It was Dr. Ambrose.

Above: Spring 2001
My beautiful children: Brandon, Cole and Karla
Below: Christmas 2004

Chapter 2

Peace. It does not mean to be in a place
where there is no noise,
trouble, or hard work. It means to be in the
midst of those things
and still be calm in your heart.

— Anonymous

AT FIRST, IT DIDN'T STRIKE ME as odd that Karla's doctor was calling my cell phone, and I answered in my usual upbeat tone, "Oh, hi, Dr. Ambrose."

With his next words, our world would never be the same.

"Mrs. Rosen, we have found something on Karla's nervous system. I've already spoken to Karla's father."

"Do you mean Rick?"

"Yes."

For him to have already called my ex-husband, who hadn't even known about what was supposed to be a routine appointment, meant something was very wrong. Rick's phone number was listed under "in case of emergency."

Before my mind could process what was happening, Dr. Ambrose told me that I needed to bring Karla back for an MRI, either now or in the morning. I started to explain that Karla's first high school dance competition was in the morning, but he cut me off.

"Mrs. Rosen," he said sternly, "Karla will not be going to her dance competition." I began to feel panicked, and pulled into the grocery store parking lot, a light drizzle still falling. Karla was listening to my side of the conversation from the backseat.

"They found a mass on her nervous system," Dr. Ambrose continued. "It's very serious. Go home and I will call you there in fifteen minutes."

As I hung up, I heard Karla ask, "Mom, what is it? What does this mean? What's wrong with me?"

Still not believing it myself, I told her, "They found something. They need you to go back now for an MRI."

Tears ran down her cheeks. She looked as if she had almost been expecting it.

Days later, Karla recounted her thoughts at that moment in her journal:

> "I DON'T THINK THAT I HAVE EVER BEEN THAT SCARED IN MY LIFE!"
> I was of course bawling because I didn't know what to think. My whole body was shaking uncontrollably and I remember I kept on asking Mom, What does this mean? What does this mean?'"

We were only minutes from home. As we pulled into the driveway, the drizzle stopped. I spotted Michael and Brandon running around the corner, laughing as they raced each other home from school. As soon as he saw my face, Michael knew something was wrong. I began to cry, and related that the doctor had told me we needed to go back immediately for an MRI. The boys ran inside to play as I tried to keep Karla calm. Before Dr. Ambrose had a chance to call back, Michael called him to find out more. All I remember is that when he hung up, he told us we needed to leave immediately for the MRI. Everything was happening too fast. I called my friend Kathi and asked her to watch my boys until Michael's parents, who only lived fifteen minutes away, could pick them up. Within five minutes we were on our way to San Antonio Hospital in Upland, about thirty minutes away.

> That ride to the hospital was miserable.
> I was feeling so many emotions that I have
> never felt before...after all, I had never
> been scared for my life before.

The trip to the hospital seemed to take forever. On the way, I called Rick and a few family members; we didn't really know anything yet for sure and didn't want to panic anyone unnecessarily. Karla called her two closest friends, Nathalie and Courtney, even though Michael and I thought she should wait until we knew more. We heard Karla sobbing in the backseat as she spoke to them, and to my surprise I could even hear, from her phone, that they were crying, too.

> I had felt a little relieved talking to my
> friends because they mean the world to me
> and that whole time I wish I could've run up
> and given them a big, giant hug. I felt so
> empty without those hugs.

When we got to Radiology, they called us in almost immediately. Since Karla was claustrophobic, they had to sedate her before the MRI, but even after taking the pill, she still didn't think she could go through with it. I recall a nurse rudely warning us that if she didn't calm down, she might have to come back in the morning when an anesthesiologist would be available. I couldn't imagine having to worry all night about what was wrong with my daughter.

As I sat there trying to calm Karla, another nurse approached her and said that she, too, was claustrophobic. "I'm going to share a secret with you, but you can't tell anyone," she whispered to us. "I can't even go to the bathroom with the door closed!" We all laughed. The nurse suggested that Karla cover her eyes before going into the tube. "I've done this before, and if I can do it, anybody can!" She was the first of the many medical professionals we encountered in the months that followed who would make our journey more bearable. Karla calmed down and agreed to do it.

All I remember about the MRI was having a towel put over my eyes, having earphones playing KIIS-FM, and zoning out lol. I got off the table and was like, 'That was it?'

I was alone outside the MRI room, and Michael was in the waiting area. About ten minutes later, they walked Karla out. She was still groggy from the sedative and needed help walking to the bathroom. We laughed as I tried holding her up while turning my head, at her insistence. In fact, she made me sing. I'll always treasure those moments of laughter because they made me believe, at least momentarily, that everything would be okay.

When we walked out of the restroom, I asked the nurse, "What do we do now?" For a few minutes I had forgotten the seriousness of why we were there, until I heard the solemn way she said, "Dr. Ambrose is on his way." I helped Karla get dressed, and we joined Michael in the waiting room. There were just two other people there, and it was eerily quiet when Dr. Ambrose arrived. He sat down next to me, across from Karla.

"There is a tumor in her brain," he explained.

"How bad is it?" I asked.

"It's ugly," Dr. Ambrose responded. He blew his nose. "Allergies," he said.

"No, that's not it," I responded. I could see how distraught he was.

Tears ran down Karla's face. I whispered in her ear, "It's going to be okay because God lives in our hearts." She responded confidently, "I know."

I couldn't comprehend what I was hearing. I suggested that we talk more in the hallway so that Karla wouldn't hear. First Michael walked out with Dr. Ambrose; I joined them a few moments later. I'll never forget the sadness in Michael's eyes as I walked toward them.

When I pressed Dr. Ambrose to tell me how serious it was, he responded, "In my lifetime, I might have one more patient like Karla."

I had to ask. "Will she die?"

"I can't tell you if she will live or die."

I fell to the ground, sobbing. It had been only two hours since that call in the car, and our lives were forever changed.

I think that my body went into shock because I couldn't do anything but sit there in awe I just couldn't believe it My mom excused herself from the room with Michael and let out the most gut-wrenching cry I have ever heard. Actually it was kind of like a scream. That was when I got really scared.

As Dr. Ambrose made arrangements for what we were to do next, we called Rick, who was on his way, and one of our pastors,

Mike, who came to the hospital with his wife Amber. As Karla and I waited, I tried to hold back my tears as we sat together. Deep down, I clung to the belief that everything would be okay.

After he had arranged for us to see a neurologist at Children's Hospital Los Angeles (CHLA) in the morning, Dr. Ambrose told us, "There is nothing they would do for her tonight, so you might as well go home, be with your family, get some rest, and head over there first thing in the morning." The words had an ominous tone.

"Go home and rest... be with your family." All I could think was *could Karla die right now?*

Karla drove home with Michael and Pastor Mike while I drove with Amber. We cried and prayed together. By the time we got home, Rick was there. We were all numb. Not knowing what to say to one another as we gathered in the kitchen and den, we just sat there speechless.

Then, all of a sudden, Karla blurted out, "Anyone hungry?" We all laughed. But no one was hungry except Karla.

We ordered in some food, and then Karla's friend Courtney called and asked Karla to come over. She didn't tell Karla that she had invited a group of Karla's closest friends to her home. Michael drove Karla over to Courtney's, and Pastor Mike met them there.

Courtney opens the door and I was totally shocked all of my friends were over! ... The whole living room was full! I remember feeling sooo loved. ...(Pastor) Mike told everyone for me exactly what was wrong, and all my girlfriends lost it ... Mike suggested that we do a prayer. It was really special hearing all of my friends saying a

part of the prayer for me and I felt so
loved. ...I remember being so happy when
I left because I knew my friends would be
there for me throughout this journey.

Back home, as the house filled with friends and the phone began ringing, I just sat there trying to make sense of everything. Though my heart was breaking, I truly did have faith.

Learned Wisdom

Faith isn't about believing everything will be all right, it's about knowing you'll be prepared when it isn't.

Above: Karla on the soccer field
with her two dads, Michael and Rick, 2003
Below: (Left) with Michael, 2002 (Right) with Rick, 2004

Chapter 3

*...God grant me the serenity to accept the
things I cannot change,
courage to change the things I can, and wisdom to know the difference.*
— Reinhold Niebuhr

AFTER A SLEEPLESS NIGHT, the following morning—when
we should have been heading to Karla's first high school dance
competition—we were instead driving to a children's hospital.
It was surreal. We heard later that the dance team did a group
prayer for Karla before they took the floor and dedicated their
performance to her, placing her poms in the spot where she
would have been on the dance floor.

It may sound strange, but I suggested to Karla that before
heading to the hospital, we stop off at the nail salon to get her
the manicure she was supposed to have gotten the day before.
Getting her nails done was one of Karla's favorite things, and I
thought it would help both of us relax before what was bound
to be a very long and stressful day. It would be one of my many
attempts to make our lives feel normal when everything around
us seemed so out of control.

When we got to the hospital, the realization that we would be surrounded by sick babies and children stunned us. It's hard to imagine a more heartbreaking place than a hospital for children.

Michael and I waited in an outer waiting room, giving Karla and Rick, who had spent the night at our house, some time together as they waited in the ER. After about an hour, they moved all of us to a small room, where we sat, paced — and, incredibly, laughed — for the next nine hours. We played with medical equipment I'm sure we weren't supposed to touch, just to keep the mood light and our minds off of what was happening. Michael, Rick, and I took turns going out to the waiting area to talk with family and friends who had shown up. At one point, Karla even went with friends to a nearby McDonald's. I soon saw that having maintained a healthy relationship with Rick was worth the patience and sacrifice.

Still, the waiting was excruciating. It felt like everything was happening so fast, yet at the same time it felt like we were in slow motion. We had so many questions and too much time to consider the "what ifs." At one point, Karla turned to me and asked, matter-of-factly, "Mom, have you ever wondered what your funeral would look like?" Taken aback, I responded with a defiant, "No!" Lightheartedly, she said, "I have." I couldn't believe we were even talking about this. The conversation ended there.

To make it worse, doctors came in once every couple hours to tell us stuff like "she might have this, but we need to look at the MRI and that might take a while. The baaad news came, however, when they told us that the tumor was deep in my brain stem and there was no way to take it out. And then they told us I would have go through chemo & radiation. I just broke down crying, trying to process it all..."

Finally the doctor entered to give us the official diagnosis: brainstem glioma, an inoperable cancerous tumor within the brain stem.

When they told us they would be admitting Karla, I recall a nurse grabbing my hand, looking me in the eye, and solemnly telling me, "Your life has changed now. Take one day at a time." The words didn't resonate with me then. Weeks later, I saw her and thanked her for that advice. She remembered our encounter, but couldn't explain why she had used those words — words she said she had never before spoken to a patient's family. I used those same words not long after while consoling another mother whose son was dying from the same illness that Karla had.

After Karla was admitted, we managed to get her into a private room where we settled in for the night. An IV was started, and we were able to clean up and get comfortable in bed. I recall how happy Karla was to be able to watch MTV! I slept in a small bed next to hers.

The next morning, Michael, Rick, and his girlfriend, Val, arrived. (It can be difficult to maintain a healthy relationship with your ex-spouse, but it's worth the patience and sacrifice. I can't even imagine what those nine hours would have been like, let alone the long months that followed, had all of us not made the choice to accept one another.) Karla awoke in great spirits. Her appetite was strong and she loved having "room service," as she called it. I was grateful for her attitude, but I couldn't help wondering how she managed to be so optimistic. I tried to be cheerful around Karla, but I was, of course, completely devastated. And when my friends Kim and Kathi showed up with pajamas for Karla, the tears flowed as I hugged them in the hallway.

When we met Dr. Jubran later that morning, it hit me: My daughter is being seen by an oncologist. Maybe it hadn't really resonated until now, or maybe I was simply in denial; either way it hit me harder than I was ready for. Dr. Jubran's less-than-warm demeanor earned her the nickname "Dr. Doom and Gloom" that day. (It would not be until later that we would learn just how wrong our first impressions were.) Within minutes came those awful words: "chemotherapy and radiation." There would be no surgery; the tumor could not be removed because of its location, the doctor said. As she outlined Karla's prospective treatment plan, Karla asked, "What about my headaches?" Dr. Jubran told Karla that her headaches would likely worsen. That seemed to shake Karla as much if not more than the news about her tumor had the day before. Karla grabbed her head and cried out. My heart sank.

When Dr. Jubran asked if we had any questions, I couldn't even speak at first. There were so many questions, yet I didn't know where to begin. Then it hit me: "My boys!" I blurted out. Before I could even begin to articulate what was going through my head, Dr. Jubran calmed my fears. No, the boys were not at risk, she said. This was not hereditary. It was an isolated case, and we couldn't have done anything to prevent it. The tumor had probably been there for years.

As she left the room, I turned to Michael and Rick and motioned for them to talk to the doctor outside. When they didn't return right away, I left Kim and Kathi with Karla and went to find them. A nurse motioned me to a closed-door room where the three were sitting. Michael and Rick just stared at me as I walked in, and the grief on their faces was something I'll never forget. With all the details I remember of that day, it surprises me that I still can't recall who said, "She's going to die."

~

Learned Wisdom

It can be difficult to maintain a healthy relationship with your ex-spouse, but it's worth the patience and sacrifice.

Chapter 4

Once you choose hope, anything's possible.
— Christopher Reeve

WITH THOSE WORDS, my knees buckled and I practically fell to the floor. Michael grabbed me and held me as I sobbed.

"How much time do I have with my daughter?" I asked through my sobs.

"One to three years," Dr. Jubran replied, emotionless.

"Is there any chance at all for survival?" I asked.

"No, I'm sorry," she said.

It just didn't seem possible. I remember feeling that I had to get out of the room. I needed to tell Karla. After all, this was her life we were talking about. Didn't she have the right to know? But Michael blocked the door, and they persuaded me to wait before telling her. Suddenly, I exclaimed, "We have to take her to New York." For years, Karla had wanted to go there, but we kept putting it off. We had just recently decided to take her and her friend Nathalie, and now I was afraid there wouldn't be time. Panic set in as I tried to figure out how to fit my daughter's lifetime of plans and dreams into one to three years.

Before we left, Dr. Jubran and I agreed that he would speak with Karla the next day, when one of our pastors could be there.

Michael and Rick made me promise I would not tell her before. I reluctantly agreed.

I'm sure Karla noticed my red, swollen eyes and tear-streaked face when I returned, but she didn't question me. I crawled into bed with her and held her tight. Holding her at that moment — knowing what I had been told but not able to share it with her — remains one of the most difficult moments of my life.

It wasn't long before word got out about Karla's tumor, and friends and family began arriving with gifts and cards. Karla wasn't feeling sick and didn't know her prognosis, so she was loving every minute of it.

That day i had looooots of visitors. The nurses were laughing because they could barely dig in and get me my IV. So i felt a lot of love that day and by the nighttime, my room was all cute and decorated.

Through all that was happening, my heart and eyes captured Michael putting his hand on Rick's shoulder to extend an open invitation into our home to see Karla. I didn't prompt him. At that moment, the resentment that had built over the years began to erode. Soon after, the door of the room opened and Brandon and Cole appeared. I hadn't seen my boys for two days. The truth is, I hadn't thought about them much; I knew they were in good hands with Michael's parents. I hugged them. Karla's face lit up, and the boys climbed into bed with her. Seeing them together I broke down and cried.

As the day went on, my pain deepened to the point where I felt as if I might explode. I tried desperately to make sense of what was going on. The only place I could go to talk aloud to God was the bathroom in the hallway. I'm not sure how many times I went there that day just to be alone to cry and pray, but this time, I fell to my knees as the tears flowed. Eyes closed, I begged God to restore my daughter's health. Still, I promised that no matter what, I would accept His will and honor Him all the days of my life. As I look back, I realize that this was the turning point for me; this was when I surrendered to God.

I dried my eyes, blew my nose, and somehow regained my composure so I could face Karla and all of our visitors. Sometimes, when I feel weak, I go back in my mind to the peace that I found that day.

Later that afternoon when Pastor Dave and his wife, Carol, came to visit, Dave told Karla he had led a prayer for her during weekend services, and then he prayed with everyone in our room. We all had a sense of peace when he left, though I knew that our next visit from a pastor would be when Dr. Jubran was telling Karla the news the following day. This weighed on me all day and night.

When everyone had left that night, including my mom and two sisters (I was adopted at birth. My older sister, Linda, was my mom's biological child. My other sister, Virginia (Ginny), was two and a half years older than I and was also adopted), it was just Karla and me. There was so much I wanted to tell her, yet I knew it had to wait. We had always had such an open relationship that it pained me to keep this from her, but I knew that for her sake I needed to wait until the time was right.

We lay there and talked for a while, and with confidence in her voice she said to me, "I'm just waiting for my miracle, because I know it's coming." We then said a prayer together, and somehow managed to fall asleep.

Karla, Saturday morning,
with Rhett, a therapy dog

Chapter 5

Sometimes you have to climb a big mountain
to see the beautiful view.
— Anonymous

IN THE MIDDLE OF THE NIGHT, I awoke to my own quiet sobbing. I was trying to hold it in so I wouldn't wake Karla in the bed next to mine. I glanced at my watch, illuminated by the moonlight coming in through the hospital window. It was 4 a.m. Monday. I still couldn't believe how much we had been through since Friday afternoon. I remember trying to pray between my tears, but there were no words.

Then, suddenly, I heard, "It's going to be okay." It was a voice I didn't recognize. My eyes were closed, and the words had such a beautiful, peaceful tone. I imagined an angel was speaking to me. "It's okay. Mom, it's going to be okay." As soon as I realized the voice was Karla's, I couldn't contain my emotions. I got into bed with her, crying uncontrollably. Though she had no idea what news was going to be revealed to her that day, she didn't question my tears. She caressed my hair and comforted me.

"It's going to be okay, Mom."

"How do you know it's going to be okay?" I asked.

"Because I talked to God," she answered confidently.

"How do you know it was God?" I asked.

"Because I know."

She went on, speaking eloquently of her faith: Jesus, sacrifice, and forgiveness. I was speechless. Though we were very involved in our church, I had come to think of Karla's recent involvement as more social than anything else. This wasn't something we had talked about, and I was surprised at how well she was able to articulate it. That was when that I realized how big a role Karla's faith was now playing in her life.

I stopped crying, amazed by this transformation in my daughter's voice and demeanor. I was convinced by her words and by her peaceful tone that she had indeed had a conversation with God, and this was when I knew that she, too, had surrendered to God.

"Promise me, Mom, that you will always have hope, even when I can't," Karla said in a tone that was soft but certain. "Promise

Karla, age 10

me, Mom?"

"I promise, Karla. I will always have hope," I answered, not fully recognizing how important those words would be, and still are, to me.

Just then, a nursing assistant came to check her blood pressure. The reading was extremely low — just 71 over 37; my heart sank once again. What was happening? Was this why Karla was asking me to have hope? Was the conversation we'd just had to prepare me for what was about to happen? So much ran through my mind as the nursing assistant left to call the nurse on duty.

My mom was trying to hold in her crying, but I kept telling her that it's OK, I'm going to be OK. And I said that you just have to put it in God's hands, and it will be OK. Then the nurse came back to check my blood pressure and I prayed hard for it to be back to normal. 'It's perfect' the nurse said. I looked over to Mom and said, 'See? I trusted God, and it was better again.' We both cried some more, then talked, then eventually fell asleep.

To this day, I can close my eyes and hear Karla's sweet voice reminding me of hope and the promise I made that day. This was the first of only two promises she would ask of me. At the time, I believed that the promise was to help her when she needed to be reminded to keep fighting and never give up. But that day never came. Now I know that the promise wasn't for her; it was for me. Karla wanted me to always have hope — even in the darkest hours — and to share that promise with those who need it most.

～

Learned Wisdom

No matter how dark your struggle, embrace every single moment of it or you will miss the opportunity to find joy and purpose.

Karla is welcomed home joyfully after her first hospital stay.

Chapter 6

God puts rainbows in the clouds so that each of us —
in the dullest and most dreary moments —
can see the possibility of hope.
— Maya Angelou

THAT NEXT MORNING, I awoke to a low, calm, matter-of-fact voice: "Mrs. Rosen, I am Doctor McComb. I am confirming that I will be doing no surgical procedures on your daughter Karla." I was barely sitting up, when my new friend, Suzy, who was also a member of our church and lived in our city, entered the room. She had hurried down from the second floor where she was working in a pediatric intensive care unit. She recently had a conversation with Dr. McComb and wanted to be by my side when he shared the last bit of medical hope with me. She sat down, and the doctor repeated what he had said to me: "My neurological team tells me there is not enough opening to insert a shunt to relieve the fluid that is building up."

Just then Suzy said, "You haven't looked at the scans yourself?"

"No," he said. "But I have confidence in my team."

"As the head of Neurology you came in here to tell this family that there is no hope, and you haven't even looked at the scans yourself?"

He then responded that he would review the scans and be back soon. Suzy couldn't believe that she had just talked to head of neurosurgery like that, putting her job in jeopardy. Within five minutes, Dr. McComb returned with his team and said, "Mrs. Rosen, it appears that there is just enough space in the ventricles to insert a shunt. We'll do this procedure today, but since Karla will be an add-on surgery, it may not be until late afternoon." He then asked permission to wake Karla, so that morning, she awoke to the news that she would, in fact, have surgery.

I woke up that morning to a whole crowd of doctors staring down at me. It was weird. That's when I first met DR. McComb and he told me that they were going to put a shunt in to relieve my headaches. This was such great news because I was told before that I was just going to have to deal with my headaches for the rest of my life. But then they said that I was going to be an add-on surgery so I'll go in any time they can fit me in. In hospitals, that's just another way of saying you're going to wait until you're bored out of your mind. To all of our surprise, one hour later they said, 'K, let's go, we're ready.' I was so shocked that I was getting in this soon. But first they had to wash my hair. lol. All they did was pour water right onto the bed! I was like 'OK, not wasting any time, I guess!' lol. But then they scrubbed it and just threw it into a towel, so it was all knotty and ratty. So we were wheeled down to the OR and Mom, Dad, Michael, and Val were all there. Before, I thought that I was ready but I was SCARED! I was shaking like crazy and crying. ...They wheeled me down the long, white hallway. The last thing I remember was being switched from the bed to the operating table. ... I didn't realize how much pain surgery was, especially when you have three incisions one in the stomach, one in the chest and one in the head. I was in so much pain it was unbelievable. I dreaded getting up to go to the bathroom because it hurt so dang bad, but they gave me lots of morphine so that put me to sleep pretty fast..

The next morning, Karla was still in great pain. Her head was sore from the insertion of the shunt, which started at the ventricles in her brain and ended in her stomach, allowing the fluids from her brain to drain naturally. Her stomach was sore from the stitches, as was her chest, where they had placed a Port-A-Cath, a device inserted under Karla's skin, through which she would receive her chemo, blood transfusions, medications, and from which blood draws would be taken during her treatments.

Before surgery, Karla's long, beautiful blonde hair was washed with antibacterial shampoo and wrapped in a towel. Now it was just a knotted mess — except for the back, which was shaved before surgery and was now covered in iodine and dried blood.

Karla couldn't eat and could barely get out of bed to use the restroom. Though she wanted more than anything to go home that day, the doctors and nurses told her she would need some time to regain her strength.

"The nurses told me that I was in too much pain to go home, but I was thinking, 'Nooo way! I'm going home today! 'So they told me that they would come back and check on me and I knew that I had to prove them wrong. Michael got Quiznos, so I sat up in my bed and ate it and I felt so good from there. The nurse walked back in and was like, Whoa! What happened to that sick girl because now she looks great! 'I was so happy! So my spirits were up really high, but then Dr. Jubran came in. She sat down with me and was like you're going to have to get radiation and chemotherapy. It was so overwhelming. And she said that I would for sure lose all of my hair. I was devastated. I tried my best not to cry but I couldn't believe it. I would never have thought that I would be this kid who gets sick with cancer and has to lose all her hair. So they left and let us get time to process it all. I got up and cleaned myself up, and even though we had just found out really bad news, at least I got to come home."

Now the impact of Karla's illness on our family dynamic began. When the doctor confirmed that Karla would lose her hair, Cole, who was lying on the bed sucking his thumb and listening, said with worry in his voice (and his thumb still in his mouth), "She's going to look like a boy." Now we had to address with our boys the seriousness of her diagnosis and talk to them about cancer.

Though the hour-long trip home from Los Angeles was difficult for Karla (she would later write in her journal "every bump felt like knives going into me"), her homecoming was wonderful. She was greeted by balloons and a huge, pink WELCOME HOME sign strung across our staircase. Our refrigerator was well stocked, the house had been cleaned — even the laundry had been done. To this day, we don't really know who did it all, but the support of our friends, family, and members of our church was apparent from the very first day of our journey.

That evening, the house was full of visitors, and Karla's room was filled with her friends. Even though she arrived home wearing pajamas, her hair pinned up, and yellow iodine all over her neck, back, and front, it didn't dampen her spirits. Not once did she complain of pain while her friends were there. She laughed as they showered her with stuffed animals, candy, and other gifts.

"Even my orthodontist cares about me!" Karla said, beaming, when she saw the vase of beautiful flowers the office had sent. That green vase still sits in our den, reminding me how much the support of all the people in our lives meant to Karla.

On that past Monday, we had been planning to tell Karla that there was no medical hope, but with the sudden news of the surgery, we changed our minds. Michael, Rick, and I agreed that we would never discuss a lack of hope because none of us, not even the doctors, could ever really be certain. Later, Karla would decide for herself that she didn't want any of us to listen to the doctors' speculations:

"If it's not happening and it's not a fact, I don't want to talk about it," she said on more than one occasion.

The day of the surgery, my niece, Kristy, came over to watch the boys. It had been raining for several days, and as Kristy turned onto our street, she saw the most vivid rainbow arching right over our house. I believe that rainbow was a sign — not just to us, but to our entire community — that one day our pain would subside and the sun would shine again.

Some months later we would find written on the laundry room whiteboard a message from Karla: "The sun always shines after it rains."

~

Courtney, Karla, and Nathalie one week after Karla's diagnosis (since Karla could not wash her hair, they braided their hair to match).

It seemed like everyone in our community was wearing a blue Amen bracelet

Chapter 7

A friend loves at all times. —
Proverbs 17:17

IN THE MIDST OF ALL OF THIS, our friend Tami paid
a visit and told us an idea that she and her husband had come
up with as a fundraiser to help pay for what we knew would be
tremendous medical-related expenses. Tami suggested that we
design our own version of those colored wristbands that had been
made so popular by Lance Armstrong, with his "Live Strong" slo-
gan. We could choose the color and the words on the bracelet.
Though we liked the idea, after Tami left, Karla changed her mind.

The following day, however, when my friends Ann and Kathi
brought the same idea to us, Karla changed her mind again:
She wanted the bracelets.

"I choose the word 'AMEN,'" Karla said without hesitation.

I was surprised by her choice; I expected it to be "let it be."
Just two weeks earlier, I had told her about something I had
learned at church: "Amen" was another way of saying "let it
be." It had reminded me of Karla because she was always saying "let it go" and "let it be." It was something she would say to
me whenever I would express frustration — often over something trivial — so it seemed logical that she would choose the
phrase for her bracelet.

"'Let it be' means 'Amen,'" Karla explained. "But if I put 'let it be' on the bracelet, no one will know that I mean 'Amen.'" Karla chose blue for her bracelet, and over the next eight weeks, we all anxiously awaited the bracelets' arrival.

Karla and I wrote an insert that would be packaged with the bracelets. It read:

> *By wearing this bracelet you are supporting*
> *a child with a life-threatening illness.*
> *Give it to God and let it be. Amen.*

I'll never forget when Ann arrived to put the first bracelet on Karla. Then Karla slipped a bracelet on Ann's wrist and then my own.

"Stuffing parties" were held all over the community to package the bracelets with the inserts, and within two weeks we had sold all 5,000 for $2 each. We ordered another 10,000, and over the next year we distributed almost all of them. Before long, we saw people wearing those blue "Amen" bracelets all over town — even people we didn't know but who had heard about Karla's story. In stores, it was fun to approach strangers who were wearing the bracelets and introduce Karla. Sometimes we didn't even tell people who we were, but just asked how they'd come to wear the bracelet. It was always interesting, and often inspiring, to hear their encouraging words. From other states — even other countries — we received emailed photos from people wearing the bracelets.

Not long after, on one of Karla's regular trips to the hospital for treatment, we stopped in to say hello to Dr. Robert Lavey, her radiation-oncology doctor. He told us that a patient about Karla's age had heard about her, and the girl and her mother were hoping to meet us. We happily obliged and headed over to the girl's room to say hello. We were not prepared for what we encountered when we walked in. Christina, who also had a brain tumor, was on a feeding tube and couldn't speak. She was lying there in a near-coma state. Her mother sat quietly at her bedside. We sat and prayed with her, and after a glance at Karla, I knew I had to give the mom my bracelet. As hard as it was to part with the first one that Karla had slipped onto my wrist, I knew it was the right thing to do. Of course, I had more bracelets at home. I often tell people that the real gift of the bracelet is being able to pass it on.

I remember one day asking Karla, "If you are to go to heaven before I want you to, what should I do with my bracelet? Should I take it off or wear it forever?"

In typical Karla fashion, she replied, "I don't care, Mom. Do whatever you want."

"Thanks, Karla. That didn't help," I said, and we both laughed. We never talked about it again.

I still wear my blue bracelet today, not because I feel I should, but because I want to.

Karla receiving her first IV chemo treatment
above, with her dad, and below, with me

Chapter 8

*We can't change the cards we are dealt, just
how we play the hand.*
— Randy Pausch

LOOKING BACK TO THE DAYS just after Karla's surgery, we saw almost immediate signs of short-term memory loss and even some personality changes.

Thankfully, the headaches had stopped, but Karla was having trouble focusing her eyes, which they told us was to be expected after surgery. Without telling Karla too many details, I did tell her that if chemo and radiation couldn't shrink the tumor, this cancer would shorten her life.

"It's the worst kind of cancer," I told her tentatively.

"I know," she said. It was clear that Karla understood the severity of her illness. I also suggested that she not go online and research her diagnosis, because the statistics were not good and a lot of current research might not be reflected in their outcomes. "If you have questions, then ask me or ask your doctors."

The coming days were an emotional roller coaster. Karla cried out to "be normal." When her friends came over, and I would hear them laughing upstairs, I would remember, for a moment, what "normal" used to be.

The week after her surgery, Karla began chemo and radiation treatments. For six weeks, Monday through Friday, we made the hour-long trip to CHLA for radiation first and then chemo. Chemo would take about four hours, and radiation would be another hour. Then we headed home, often in bumper-to-bumper traffic. It was exhausting. When we finally arrived home, attempting the simple task of helping my first-grader son with his basic homework felt overwhelming and often became a balance that I couldn't master. At times, the pressure of caring for Karla made trying my best to keep everything else as normal as possible impossible.

I hated being at the hospital; the stench of sickness was everywhere. The bathrooms smelled of dirty diapers. Eventually, we got used to it — just as you get used to anything, however awful, when you're exposed to it day after day.

Still, it took weeks before I was able to eat at the hospital. But not Karla — almost from the start, she enjoyed being able to order off the hospital menu any time. She had saved her first hospital menu as a memento of her hospital stay. She even ate while she was getting chemo. If she ate, I tried to eat with her, even if I wasn't hungry, but if she didn't want to eat, I wouldn't eat, either — regardless of how hungry I was.

Karla disliked chemo, but she never complained while we were there. Radiation was another story. The mouthpiece she had to wear was so uncomfortable that it made her dread the process, even though the actual radiation lasted only about ten minutes. A special pillow was molded to her head so the radiation could be precise. Even though she hated the procedure, she loved Dr. Lavey. He always gave Karla hope and made her feel as if she were his only patient.

In fact, many of the nurses spoiled Karla. From the start, she had greeted everyone with an infectious smile and a bubbly "Hi!" When we arrived, the nurses would greet her with a big "Karla!" We had girl-gabbing sessions, ice-cream parties and movie reviews, and we came to think of many of the nurses as friends. One of them, Alison, told me, "I feel selfish saying this, but we love it when Karla comes into chemo." I thanked her for loving my baby.

One of the things I cherished during this time was walking arm in arm with Karla. One day while we sat in chemo, a woman visiting her daughter came over to say, "I have been watching you and your daughter and how beautiful you are together." I felt Karla and I were becoming best friends again — a feeling I hadn't had in a while.

Two weeks after her surgery, Karla announced her goals: to maintain her grades in school — which were back to straight A's — and to stay active. Karla was always a top student, and she was determined not to let cancer get in the way of that. She accepted that she would not return to school for the rest of her freshman year and that she would be on the home/hospital school program. We were all hopeful that she would be able to return to school in the fall.

As far as school goes, I have no stress whatsoever because I have a home tutor now and I feel confident that everything will be fine. I am homeschooling for the rest of the year only taking geometry and English. And I get PE credit for doing anything physical, like cleaning my room! Before, I was really freaked out about homeschooling because I was scared about becoming all antisocial, but now I'm totally cool with it because I know that won't happen, and plus, for the next 6 months I don't have to deal with dumb, immature high school drama!

Karla also decided that, in addition to returning to dancing, she wanted to take up soccer again. She had given it up last summer after we told her she needed to choose between soccer and dance; doing both would have been just too much, especially during her first year of high school. In fact, I was disappointed that she had chosen to give up soccer, simply because she was so good at it, but now everything had changed. We would let her set her goals as high as she wanted and encourage her every step of the way.

Last night Nicole came over in her Stampede (soccer) gear and for some reason really inspired me to get onto that team! So that is a new goal that I'm going to add to my list!

Karla was attempting to keep her life as normal as possible and setting new goals, and I was doing the same. Just before Karla was diagnosed, I had been asked to serve on a committee to help plan an upcoming women's retreat for our church. And though I was told that everyone would understand if I stepped down, I knew that doing so would be a mistake. I knew, somehow, that holding on to our regular routines and responsibilities — as much as we could — would help us get through our days. If our lives were consumed with cancer and our days defined by hospital trips, then we would lose a part of ourselves and what gave our lives joy and purpose in the first place. So I hung on to those responsibilities and encouraged everyone in the family to do the same.

I recall sitting in the hospital waiting room and talking to a mother whose daughter's cancer had come back after being in remission. She told me how important it was to keep it "normal" in the house — even having her daughter do chores when she felt up to it. Some months later, when Karla was feeling good, I asked her to do the dishes on several occasions. I hated asking, and felt guilty being upstairs reading while she was in the kitchen. I remember coming down to sit at the kitchen table so that I could be with her while she was at the sink.

Another of Karla's goals was to attend her school's Winter Formal dance, which was about a month after her diagnosis. Much to our surprise, she received a flower announcing she had been nominated for Freshman Princess. Of course, she was ecstatic, and though I was happy for her, I was also a bit worried: there were side effects from the steroids and chemo, including weight gain and a skin rash. I continued to reassure her about how beautiful she was. I wanted her to go to the dance and have a wonderful time. I wanted her to have all of the experiences she was supposed to have: to graduate from high school and college, to get married, and have her own children. I wanted her to be able to live life.

I have completed nine days of radiation... almost two whole weeks are already over! I also get my last day of (round one) chemo today so that I have officially been on it one week. Although this whole process is going by really slow, it is going by very fast at the same time. I know that I'm going to be looking back in six weeks and go WOW! I'm done! The chemo hasn't hit me yet and I'm really hoping that my body takes to it well, which they said it should because I am so strong and healthy. The only side effect that's hit me really bad is, well, I don't know what it's called, but I can get into the psycho moods and I freak out not just anytime, but when people want to come see me all the time I get no rest or time to myself and it drives me absolutely insane

Oh, and another side effect is my eating. lol. Gosh like I really needed more food than I already eat! I'm hungry all the time and I'm always thinking about food. I'm trying to learn to control my eating without starving myself, but it's really hard. Anyways, Winter Formal is... on February 12!! AND I GOT NOMINATED FOR FRESHMAN PRINCESS! I'm so excited! Me, Court and Adam are going together so I know that we're going to have so much fun! Now me and Court need to go out dress, jewelry, shoe (and for me, wig) shopping. It will all work out perfectly."

Karla usually displayed incredible strength, humor, and a positive attitude under even the most challenging circumstances, especially for her visitors, but there were also many times when she would snap at me or demand to be left alone. I wanted to always be compassionate; I knew that the steroids she was on had some negative side effects, like drastic mood swings, and we were also often exhausted and irritable after long days at the hospital. But sometimes, as would be expected, she was just feeling sorry for herself, and she took out her frustrations on her brothers and me. While my heart was breaking for her, it was difficult not to lose my patience.

On January 23, just a couple weeks after her diagnosis, I wrote about it in my journal:

Snapping at me is what she does. She called us four times during breakfast because she was starving. She snapped because it didn't have enough butter and why wasn't I bringing it quick enough.

I recall one particularly difficult "steroid moment" that occurred about a month after Karla was diagnosed. While we were shopping at Target, she decided she wanted me to buy a set of baking dishes for her to give to her father. The box was opened and missing a dish, but she insisted that I buy it. I tried reasoning with Karla, but she started crying and yelling. I finally had to put down the other items we were going to buy and walk out. I couldn't recall ever having had to do that before — not even when she was a toddler. She followed me without a word and was quiet the entire way home. We both hated those steroids.

The stress on our family was immense. Shortly before Karla's diagnosis, Cole had started going to preschool for three hours a day, three days a week. Now he was going full-time (his school's administrators were kind enough to offer the extra hours at no additional charge), but Cole would beg me not to leave when I dropped him off in the morning. I hated having to leave him all day, but there was no way I could stay with Karla during her treatment and entertain Cole at the hospital, too. Even though friends often called and asked how they could help, it was difficult for me to ask them to take my boys for the day; however, I soon accepted, as it became impossible to take them with us.

I'll never forget the one time I wound up taking both boys to the hospital with me when Karla was undergoing chemo. She was irritable that morning, Brandon wasn't behaving, and Cole had a cough, which meant that he had to wear a facemask while on the chemo floor (which he refused to do). The boys began taunting each other, so I took them down to the first floor to get them some fast food. As they started pushing each other in line (and pushing me to the edge of my sanity), in walked Robyn Westbrook, the hospital psychologist with whom I had become acquainted. After we got the food and walked back to the waiting room where I was going to leave them to eat while I checked on Karla, the food fight started. As I tried to reason with the boys,

Dr. Westbook offered to stay with them while I went to see Karla. She managed to calm the boys down, and when I returned, Cole agreed to wear the mask so we could all sit with Karla while she finished her chemo. That was the last time I took both boys with me while Karla was undergoing treatment.

With those daily back-and-forth trips to the hospital, I was also unable to keep up with normal household chores. Without fuss or complaint, Michael was incredibly supportive and took on the role of "Mr. Mom," helping with the boys and household duties, but there were days when he would come home from work and point out that we were low on groceries or that the laundry wasn't done. Sometimes, after a long day, I would just want to check out for the evening.

Though the boys were still too young to fully understand what was happening, they were certainly old enough to know that something was very wrong with their sister. They began asking questions.

"How sick is Karla?"

"Is she sicker than Papa?" They were referring to my father, who had died of leukemia less than two years earlier. When I answered yes, they asked, "Is Karla going to die?" I explained to them that their sister was very sick, but that we must never lose hope or faith in God — no matter what the outcome.

Later that month, it was a wonderful surprise for the boys when Brandon's principal, Rob Clements, who didn't know Karla personally but had heard how courageously she was taking on her illness, wrote the following in his February newsletter:

...this young woman is faced with adversity others only pray they never have to face. It was not the circumstance, but her response to the circumstance, that was so important. She has rightfully taken her position as one of my heroes.

～

Learned Wisdom

Get to know your loved ones now, and don't let the daily distractions of life prevent you from learning who they truly are, because no one can predict when they might be taken from you.

Above: Karla, just after getting her head shaved
Below: Courtney, Adam, and Karla at their Winter Formal

Chapter 9

Out of difficulties grow miracles.
— Jean de la Bruyere

THE DATE OF WINTER FORMAL was fast approaching. Karla was going with two of her best friends, Courtney and Adam. I knew the three of them would have a great time together.

To be honest, however, while Karla was looking forward to it, I knew all the preparation it would take and I was dreading her going. We were still making daily trips to the hospital for chemo and radiation, and, as if we weren't already under enough stress, we would need to find a dress. Long before Karla became ill, I had come to dread shopping with my teenage daughter. What happened to my dream of mother and daughter having fun, laughing and trying on clothes together? Whatever I picked out for her to try on was "ugly." What I thought was "in" was definitely "out." What I thought looked great on her was — how did she put it? — "I hate it!" So I expected that going shopping with a teenager on steroids would be torture!

Fortunately, Rick offered to take Karla to look for a dress after chemo one day, and I accepted his offer. For the first time, I could take a day off from the hospital and catch up on, well, life. Incredibly, Karla came home with the first dress she'd tried on at the first store they'd gone to (wouldn't that figure?). Though she was about thirty pounds over her normal weight, and wanted to cover up the port on the left side of her chest, the blue, beaded dress looked stunning on her. At that point I thought maybe getting Karla to this dance would be easier than I had feared. I was wrong.

The doctor said Karla's hair would likely start falling out soon, and we had been talking about cutting her hair before the dance. She was petrified of having chunks of hair fall out in front of people. Yet the thought of shaving her head was overwhelming for her, too. On top of everything else, Karla was still experiencing double vision and mood swings — and then there was the insomnia. We were told it was caused by the steroids needed during radiation to reduce the swelling in her brain. Sleep medication didn't help.

Around the same time, Karla was given a gift basket that included the book *Bethany Hamilton, Soul Surfer,* the true story of the champion surfer who lost an arm in a horrific shark attack and then came back to surf again. Karla read it in one night. It was incredibly inspiring to her. She slept soundly that night — and awoke with clear vision!

In the morning, she told us she was ready to shave her head.

"If Bethany Hamilton can go back to surfing without her arm, then I can shave my hair," Karla announced. "I can't control the cancer, but I can take control of my hair falling out." So that day we went wig shopping.

We wound up at an awful, stale, wig store. None of the wigs resembled Karla's hair, and she was closing up and getting irritable. I tried to keep her spirits up, but deep down I wanted to scream. The last place I wanted to be was in that store looking for a wig for my teenage daughter.

After seeing so many fake-looking synthetic wigs, Karla decided that she wanted a human-hair wig. These were much more expensive (nearly $2,000), but family members and friends had offered to pay for any wigs that Karla might need. At first, it was difficult for us to accept financial help. Michael made a good living in logistics management and had a generous insurance plan, and Rick also contributed to Karla's expenses.

We recognized that we were in much better financial shape than many other people facing similar challenges, but it didn't take long before it became clear that the hardship would be greater than we had anticipated. We were constantly at the pharmacy for new meds — when one didn't work, another would be prescribed — some of them costing hundreds of dollars for a few weeks' supply. The deductibles for doctors' visits and lab work, medical supplies, new clothes for Karla's changing body — were all adding up quickly, so when the offers came from friends and family to help pay for Karla's wigs, we gratefully accepted. A friend also reminded me how giving to someone in need also helps the heart of the giver. This made being on the receiving end a little easier. And it taught me that in order to be a good giver, you must be willing to receive.

> I've been fitting for my wigs and getting them all setup because I'm shaving my hair! I know that I'm ready, though, because I've been preparing myself for this a long time. Plus, I had a dream that chunks of my hair started to fall out and it was awful! I woke up crying."

The following day, we went to a salon that specialized in human-hair wigs. The experienced stylist calmed Karla's nerves, listened to what she wanted, and had her try on some wigs. The wig would be ordered the next day and shipped overnight so Karla would be able to shave her hair and have plenty of time to style her wig before the dance. A few days later, we got a call that her wig was in and we rushed over. When the stylist pulled it out of the box, we were speechless. The wig's color and style could not have been more different than what we had discussed. Karla looked at me as the stylist put it on her, and her eyes welled up with tears. I didn't want to say anything, but I was screaming inside. Then Karla started crying and said, "This is not the wig I ordered."

The stylist responded coldly, "Sorry, but this is what you ordered." She offered to lend us a sample wig for the dance. On top of our disappointment and frustration, the stylist pressured us to hurry. "You're going to have to make a decision or go in the next room, because my next client is going to be here soon," she said, sounding irritated. I was stunned that someone could be so uncaring when dealing with a young girl with cancer.

We went into a small waiting room and tried on some sample wigs. Karla was crying in frustration and disappointment, but we accepted the sample wig out of desperation.

When we got home, we called a friend who had dealt with a similar situation a few years ago. She recommended a wig boutique that we went to the next day. While there was no longer enough time before the dance to order a human-hair wig, the saleswoman suggested a straight, long, blonde synthetic wig. While it didn't look real, at least it was close to Karla's natural color.

The wig was shipped the following day. That evening, Karla decided she was ready to shave. A salon was out of the question — she didn't want anyone there but the stylist and me. Fortunately, our friend Julie, who is a stylist and had done Karla's hair for some time, agreed to do it. By the time we got there it was late. Karla was calm, content with her decision. Then she asked something that surprised me: she wanted Julie to wash and blow-dry her hair one last time. Julie agreed, but it was like torture watching my daughter's silky blonde hair being washed and blown, knowing that I might never see it again. The minutes felt like hours.

Julie put Karla's hair in a ponytail and cut away. Then she buzzed it all the way to the scalp. It was difficult for Julie because Karla's head and face were covered in a rash from the steroids. My eyes filled with tears as I watched. "It's only hair!" Karla said, trying to comfort us. Karla smiled during the entire process, and even smiled for a photo, completely bald, before putting on what we called her "Barbie" wig.

It was late by the time we got home, and I dreaded what the next day would bring. Would the boys freak out when they saw their sister bald? Would Karla regret her decision to cut it off? Before going to sleep I wrote in my journal:

Karla went to sleep bald. Thank you, God,
for getting me through this difficult day,
and giving me one more day with all my kids.
Amen.

The following morning, Cole jumped into bed with us as we read the article about Karla's diagnosis in the local paper, *The Champion.* A reporter had come to interview us several days earlier, and we decided it was time to tell our story to the community. The article captured Karla's positive attitude, hope, and courage as she faced a challenge that no fourteen-year-old should ever have to take on. A photo of Karla and her brothers taken just one month before her diagnosis accompanied the article. In it, Karla spoke of how important the support of her family and friends was to her — and also of her faith.

"I am definitely calm because I know God will take care of it," Karla was quoted as saying. She expressed her gratitude for all of the gifts, notes of encouragement, and the prayer quilt made for her at church — with a silent prayer said as each square knot was tied. She spoke of "taking control" by cutting her own hair, and of wanting to help provide comfort to children at the hospital who were not as fortunate.

A mention of the Amen bracelets sent orders soaring, and the article invited anyone interested in receiving updates about Karla to subscribe to the church website. The article unleashed a flood of good wishes from friends as well as strangers. And the reporter, Marianne Napoles, became a friend as she continued to chronicle Karla's journey.

Just as we finished reading, Cole grabbed the paper and ran down the hall to Karla's room to show it to her.

"Sissy, sissy, we're in the newspaper!" Cole yelled in excitement. While Karla read the article, I asked Cole, "Do you notice anything about your sissy?"

"Yeah, she doesn't have any hair." And then he continued to talk about the article. I had told the boys the night before that Karla was cutting off her hair, so they would be prepared. I even brought the wig out to let them touch and feel it. And Cole's nonchalant response was exactly what Karla needed to hear. The same girl who insisted she would never come out of her room without a wig was now walking around the house bald — and was fine with it. That day, she put on her new wig and went to watch her dance team compete at a nearby high school and was smothered in hugs.

Still, Karla was not satisfied that this "everyday" wig would be appropriate for the dance, which was now one week away. Human-hair wigs can be styled, curled, and pinned up, but there are limits to what you can do with a synthetic wig. After looking online, we found a huge wig store in Los Angeles. We were relieved to see all kinds of people, young and old, buying wigs. We found a beautiful synthetic wig that had been styled and would look great with her gown. The order was rushed and due to arrive on Thursday — two days before the dance.

Next, we shopped for shoes and accessories. Even though Karla was beginning to lose her balance, she insisted on heels. I asked my friend Kathi to go shopping with us and act as a mediator. Except for Karla's occasional outbursts of frustration that she looked "ugly" because of her rash, things were proceeding smoothly. We visited a makeup artist at Nordstrom, and after spending a few hundred dollars on cosmetics to cover her rash, Karla looked great. More important, she felt great, but how would we recreate this ourselves at home before the dance?

Then, out of the blue, a friend of ours called and told us that her neighbor had read the newspaper article about Karla and wanted to know whether there was anything she could do to help our family. The woman was an esthetician, so it was perfect! I asked if she would come over before the dance and help cover Karla's rash and do her makeup. I was beginning to get better about taking people up on their offers of help; I came to realize that we couldn't make it through this journey without the help and support of the people around us. Rebecca came immediately to give Karla a facial and to practice her makeup before the big night.

The wig showed up as we had hoped, and another friend came over to help thin it out and style it for us. I watched from bed; I was coming down with the flu and felt miserable. I suppose it was only a matter of time before the stress and exhaustion caught up with me. I thought we were ready for tomorrow — the big day — but I awoke the next morning to Karla whispering, "Mom, I don't like my wig. I want it styled different." I was so sick I didn't even have the energy to argue. I told Karla to get me the phone book and chose a salon at random. I knew all the salons would be mobbed with high school girls getting ready for the dance, plus, we needed someone with expertise in styling wigs, but the first salon I happened to call did have someone available, and as it turned out he was also a stylist for City of Hope, a nearby hospital that specializes in cancer patients. Pete was wonderful, and Karla left the salon thrilled with her newly styled wig. We got her nails done, and Rebecca came over to do her makeup. I can still feel the stress of that day as I write this, but I can also still feel the joy of seeing Karla walk down the stairs looking as beautiful as she did. Her dad joined us as we took photos of her and then dropped her off at Courtney's house where the limo was to pick up the group. When Rick offered to pick up Karla from Courtney's later and to be on-call if she wanted to go home early, this was the first time being separated from her overnight was just fine. I was so exhausted that I don't even recall falling into bed that night.

The entire stressful week of getting Karla to feel "normal" again was one of the "worth every moment" times of her journey. That night, she wrote these prayers that we later found in her room:

God... Thank You For

-giving me the perfect night
-making me feel like a princess
-winning princess
-my mom - for putting in all the stress and money to let me go to the dance
-Michael - for being so loving and patient towards me and the willingness to buy me anything for the dance that I needed
- My dad - for being there for me and waiting so that I could go home when I was ready and for just loving me so much
- letting me get my dress, shoes, purse, and jewelry all the very first time we went looking for them
- Chloe - for being by my side the entire night
- Adam - for being the perfect date
-Court - for being the perfect bestfriend
-letting the wig Jennifer had be bad so that we could go to Wilshire Wigs and ... so that we

could go to the Grand Avenue Salon and
meeting Pete so that he could make my wig
and style look perfect
-Becca - for saving my skin as much as she could
and for doing a perfect job on my makeup
-letting me be in the newspaper so that I could
inspire other people
-all of our friends who have given us prayers,
support comfort, gifts, and love
-having my dad's girlfriend move out so that
my dad can start working towards having a very
positive and happy outlook on and just normal
life
-making my dad feel better so that he has more
energy so that he doesn't get depressed about
things
-my family-for caring so much and for always
being there
-my doctors-for being the very best out there
and for treating me so well
-my nurses-for being so nice and friendly and
for taking such good care of me
-my brothers-for being so good through all this
and   forgiving me so much love and care
-for letting all of my appointments, schedules,
and errands work out perfectly throughout the
last four weeks
-my two beautiful homes, everything in them,
and all of the other things that I have that most
kids don't

-all of the little things that you do everyday
-letting Me be the one to bring our community
together and inspire them
-for giving Me the strength to get through
this and to letMy body take to the treatments
so well
-for letting Mediscover My tuMor when I did
so that I can treat it and get rid of it

When I read Karla's neatly printed list, I was struck by the number of times she used the word "perfect." It was a word I don't think I had used since Karla was diagnosed, but Karla used it all the time.

Even though there were times when she was frustrated and upset, I don't think Karla ever asked, "Why me?" She never felt sorry for herself. If anything, she wondered why she was the recipient of so much love, so many gifts. Instead of being angry with God, she was thankful for the strength she was given to handle this challenge. This was, and still is, one of Karla's most beautiful gifts to all of those around her — her ability to look for, and find, the good in everyone and everything.

Learned Wisdom

To be a good giver, you must also be willing to receive.

 # Chapter 10

Love is the great miracle cure.
— Louise Hay, Author of *You Can Heal Your Life*

An email sent to our friends, family and church community:

Email Update #2
Feb. 14, 2005

Hey Everyone!
Thank you so much for your amazing amounts of thoughts and prayers! I wish there were a way to give back all of the love and support I have received!
My treatments are going very well and I'm feeling great considering the amounts of energy that I have (which alter from exhaustion to somewhat normal). I'm also starting to get a few more side effects such as muscle aches, mouth sores and loss of appetite. But still no weakness or vomiting, so I'm still very strong!
Also my faith in God always lifts my spirits, and attitude is half the battle! But again, I can't say thank you enough to everyone for being there for my family and me, because my family needs just as much support as I do.

I've already finished four weeks of radiation, so right now my prayer request would be that my body continues to take the treatments well and that at the next MRI, God will show everyone how amazing his miracles really are!
All my love,
Karla

Two weeks after she wrote this update, Karla faced her next challenge. She developed a high fever that required her to be hospitalized for a week. When we returned home, her appetite seemed to dwindle daily and she had severe nausea. She was admitted again, and this hospital stay turned into four weeks. They finally diagnosed her with severe pancreatitis, esophagitis, gastritis, and typhlitis (a serious bowel infection).

I had never seen her in so much pain. She was placed on "NPO," which meant she was not allowed any food or liquids by mouth — not even an ice cube! She was fed intravenously, and began receiving daily shots to boost her immune system.

This time, Karla asked friends not to visit; for the first time, we watched our daughter slip into a depression. Her weight was

Michael visiting Karla during her month stay in the hospital

up, she was still bald, and her skin was blotchy from the lipids being fed to her intravenously twelve hours a day. Every morning between 2 a.m. and 4 a.m., a nurse would draw her blood and we would anxiously await the results. The normal range was 100–300; Karla's numbers hovered around 1,600.

The first few days were rough: Karla fought and cried and wouldn't communicate. One day I gave in to her cries and went to get her an ice cube. I couldn't watch her suffer like this. I knew it could cause her numbers to shoot up, but I thought it would bring her a moment of relief. Once again, she surprised me. "No, I don't need it. I can do this," Karla said firmly. I knew Karla wanted to take control of the little she could.

During that month-long stay, I slept at the hospital every night but two. While I was gone, Michael not only took care of the boys and the house but he was also wonderful with Karla. When it became evident that this latest hospital stay would be a long one, he bought Karla a laptop so she could be connected to the outside world. Also, to help brighten her spirits, he would bring the boys to visit her whenever he could.

Kassey, Karla, Chloe, and Courtney,
just being girls, after Karla's release

Though Michael and Karla had their ups and downs over the years, she appreciated all the love and attention Michael was showing her. For Valentine's Day, Karla got him a card in which she handwrote: "You have made me realize how much I really do love you and how much you are really there to love and support me, too ... I think that God put me through this to bring us closer together."

As much as I missed Michael and the boys during that month at the hospital, I also missed my bed and the cleanliness of my own home. Hospitals feel so unclean to me. I particularly hated showering there. There was one bathroom and two showers designated just for parents. It often smelled, and there was no place to set my clean clothes or towels. Mostly, though, I worried that Karla would need me while I was gone.

Even when Karla began feeling better, she still insisted on no visitors. She said she didn't want anyone to see her so sick because then they would feel sorry for her. The only exceptions were her brothers — whom Michael would bring as often as he could, and this always made her smile — and her friend Courtney. Once, her nurse, Tommy, allowed us to break the rules and let Courtney spend the night in our hospital room. The girls stayed up late, and to this day I can still hear them sharing stories and that incredible laughter. I'm so thankful that Tommy knew that breaking the rules that night was better than any medicine they could have put through Karla's IV.

One night I gathered my nightclothes and headed to the parent showers. As I passed the nurses' station, I noticed a monitor positioned in the middle that showed a very low heart rate. As I looked over to the right, I saw one bed centered in a room instead of the usual two. Several people were gathered around the bed. Then it hit me: someone's child is dying. My heart sunk.

I couldn't wait to get back to the room to see Karla, just to hold her. I didn't tell her what I had seen. About an hour later, while Karla was in the bathroom, I heard a commotion in the hallway: people running, patient room doors being quickly shut, awful

cries. Then there was silence. I felt numb. Karla opened the bathroom door, looked at me and asked, "Mommy, what's wrong?"

I chose to tell her what was happening. She didn't freak out or
cry. We sat down and prayed for the family. We didn't know who
the child was, but it didn't matter; we closed our eyes and prayed.

The next morning I awoke before Karla, as I always did. I looked
forward to the quiet, peaceful time to read my Bible, to find the
peace I needed to start another day. With Karla still sleeping, I
headed to the dreaded showers. As I approached the room on the
right, an awful smell hit me, something stronger than the scent of
bleach. When I looked inside, I saw the empty room, the bed in
the center stripped down, confirming what I already knew from
the night before. A floor fan blew, and I knew they were sanitiz-
ing the room. It was the smell of death in a hospital. I also knew
at that moment that, if and when God said it was Karla's time,
and I had a choice, I did not want my child to die in the hospital.

Karla's next MRI was scheduled for April 7. It was the first since
her treatment had started, so everyone was anxiously awaiting the
results. We put out a prayer request for that date; I was told later
that our church was filled with family and friends and that what
had begun as a solemn event turned into a joyful prayer celebration. We were heartened to discover later that people all over our
community — and beyond — paused that morning to honor and
pray for Karla. The hospital stay had been rough on all of us, but
the day of her MRI, Karla awoke feeling better and with a bright
outlook. It made us believe, once again, that anything was possible.

Church email update, written by our friend and senior pastor's wife Carol:

Email Update #6
April 7, 2005

*What a wonderful day this has been. I have just returned
from spending the day with Karla, Ruthe, Mike, and Rick.
We have wonderful and awesome news to share with you!*

After reviewing the MRI that was taken today, the doctor came into the room with a big smile on her face and informed us that the tumor is smaller... significantly smaller!!! Thank you, God!!

When I walked into the room this morning, it was so encouraging to see a bright and smiling face on Karla. Those beautiful eyes were sparkling, and I loved seeing that. She is feeling so much better than even just yesterday, and the nausea was gone. ... When it was time to go downstairs for the MRI, Karla didn't want the wheelchair. She wanted to walk! And Ruthe said that it was the first time Karla had been walking in the two weeks since she has been in the hospital this time. How exciting that was for us to see. It was a good day!

Our next goal is to see Karla coming home.

We were all thrilled by the results of the MRI. One week later, on April 14, Karla was released from the hospital. It had been four weeks since she'd had a glass of water, and she was ordered to stay on TPN (intravenous food), allowing only clear liquids, for another month after she came home. She hated being on the IV twelve hours a day. Though the doctors were reluctant to send her home with pancreatitis, three days after her discharge, Karla was out with friends playing miniature golf. Karla's perspective on the simple things in life changed like I never could have imagined — especially for a teenager!

That first weekend home felt so, well, wonderfully normal! We gardened, visited with friends, and the boys played in the pool.

And I didn't take a moment for granted.

Chapter 11

The first duty of love is to listen.
— Paul Tillich

JUST FOUR MONTHS AFTER Karla was diagnosed, we heard that one of my dear friends, Nikki, who was only thirty-four and the mother of two little girls, had been diagnosed with breast cancer. The news was devastating. Friends had known for some time but had been reluctant to tell me, especially while Karla was in the hospital. Just a few weeks earlier, Nikki and I had been talking over coffee, and she was the one comforting me. When I heard the news and called Nikki, we reflected back on that conversation.

Just a week after being told of her diagnosis, Nikki was scheduled to have a double mastectomy. Karla had requested a prayer quilt for Nikki from church, like the one that had been given to her in the hospital. The night before Nikki's surgery, after Karla's chemo appointment, we brought the quilt over. Nikki's husband, Rob, and I were deeply touched as Karla and Nikki held hands and commiserated together. We were struck by the beauty of a fourteen-year-old with brain cancer comforting a mother of two with breast cancer.

Karla tried to give Nikki an idea of what to expect when she got to the hospital, based on what she had gone through, like the Port-A-Cath that would be inserted in her chest to deliver the chemo, and tips on how to deal with the resulting nausea. In the weeks and months that followed, their friendship grew as they held on to each other for support. Sometimes Karla even scolded Nikki, like when she saw her walking outside barefoot: "What if you cut your foot and get an infection?"

Not long after Nikki shaved her head, she and Karla laughed and had fun as they tried on Karla's wigs. They felt comfortable walking around bald in front of each other. I'll never forget sitting outside on the patio, playing Scrabble with my daughter and my dear friend — both of them utterly bald. That time together wasn't about cancer or illness — it was about friends being together, laughing, and playing a game on a summer's afternoon.

More than anything, Karla shared with Nikki her faith, and how to let go of things that are not in your control.

"These are your darkest days," Karla told Nikki gently. "I promise it's going to get better."

Karla inspired Nikki to shave her head after she was diagnosed with breast cancer. Nikki's girls, Ellie, 1, and Maddie, 3, sported scarves to support their mom.

Chapter 12

"Promise me you'll give faith a fighting chance.
And when you get the choice to sit it out or dance,
I hope you dance."
— Tia Sillers, "I Hope You Dance"

DURING THESE STRESS-FILLED MONTHS, the support and love we received from others helped us get through each day.

Our church organized a meal-delivery schedule with friends, neighbors, and people we barely knew bringing over dinner each night. Close friends offered to watch the boys and even took them to baseball and soccer practices. Rick's involvement on the Kawasaki motocross team led to a fundraiser in Karla's name that brought in thousands of dollars — selling limited-edition colored bands with each of the top riders' names — to help with our medical expenses. My sisters, Ginny and Linda, helped too, raising several thousand dollars by holding multiple candle fundraisers for us.

Another source of support was Karla's school dance team. She had many close friends on the team, and even the girls she didn't know had rallied around her as well. During Karla's four-week hospital stay, I got a call from Michelle, another mom whose daughter was on the team. She and the team advisor,

Judy, wanted to know how we felt about the school organizing a performance to honor Karla, with the proceeds donated to our family. Though Karla was honored to have her team's support, she was very uncomfortable with a dance in her name.

"How about a dance that goes on to help other kids like me?" Karla suggested. We imagined an annual dance that would benefit a teen whose family was going through a struggle similar to ours. Aside from the financial contribution to help with the many costs associated with battling a life-threatening illness, the dance would be a vehicle for the child's peers to show their love and support.

Karla with dancers at the first Dance of Hope, 2005

Karla with Ricky Carmichael at the Las Vegas Supercross, June 2005

"And next year I will dance a solo!" Karla said with absolute confidence.

Just weeks later, in May 2005, the sold-out Dance of Hope became a reality. The two-night performance showcased dancers not only from Karla's high school, but also other schools in our district as well as dance studios from all over the community. It was an inspiring and emotional evening. Michael was out of town, but several family members attended. It was the first time since her diagnosis that my birth mother, Melinda, whom I had found at age nineteen, had seen Karla.

Karla had been dreading the evening; she was insecure about being out in public because of her rash and weight gain, but I saw her insecurities fade as she went onstage to accept flowers and thank the audience. Many of those in attendance told us afterward that Karla, beaming with hope and confidence, had stolen the show.

Months later, Karla made me promise that the Dance of Hope would continue. We both had realized how important it is for teenagers facing serious illnesses to see that, regardless of how they look or feel, they are loved, and their friends and the community are there for them. And I'm grateful to say that, with the help of many others, we have been able to carry on the tradition and honor a different child every year since Karla took the stage.

~

Learned Wisdom

If your heart's desire is to help someone in need, just do it, and know you are making a difference.

Karla happily settles into her new room.

Chapter 13

The more you praise and celebrate your life,
the more there is in life to celebrate.
— Oprah Winfrey

AFTER HER ENCOURAGING MRI and subsequent checkups, Karla's doctors said she would have no physical limitations during the summer; what she could do was up to her and depended on her strength. It was such exciting news! Karla wanted to do it all: wakeboarding, dancing, playing soccer — and, of course, catching up on her social life. I was a bit worried she would overdo it, but after all she had been through, I couldn't consider holding her back.

With Karla on a break from chemotherapy, and with her ability to eat restored, the next few weeks felt sensationally normal. We enjoyed our time together as a family, boating, shopping, and just being at home.

Not long after, Karla started a two-week-on, two-week-off chemo schedule, with both IV and pills. She had been keeping up on schoolwork, and we fully expected her to be back in school full-time in the fall. She was ready and determined to beat cancer.

That summer, we created memories that will last me a lifetime. We took two wonderful vacations up north to Clear Lake and Lake Havasu, where we boated and saw family and friends. Seeing Karla wakeboard again was a gift. The trip felt so normal, in fact, that we even bickered a couple of times — just like a normal teenager does with her "annoying" parents. There were times during that trip that I almost forgot that cancer was a part of our lives.

Karla was feeling so good that Michael and I felt secure enough to take a four-day trip, on our own, to Hawaii. Karla stayed with Courtney's family while we were gone, and when we got back, we found that Karla's friends had given her wig a "new look," styling it and pinning the bangs to the side. Karla loved getting the much-needed chance to spend time with her friends, feeling good and just being normal.

That summer we had a visit from an old friend, Jim, who had moved with his family to Hawaii to manage a resort. Somehow, we began talking about Bethany Hamilton, the teenage surfer whose book had inspired Karla and given her the courage to shave her head. Jokingly, I told Jim that if Bethany, who lived in Hawaii, ever visited his hotel, to please get her autograph for Karla.

A few weeks later, the phone rang and Karla answered. It was Bethany. Jim had somehow contacted her family, and she wound up talking to Karla for about fifteen minutes. Karla was ecstatic. Bethany invited our family to come to a surfing competition in Southern California where she would be competing. Karla, Cole, and I showed up and got to watch her surf. After the competition, these two teenage girls, who had gone through so much in their short lives, sat down and talked. It was an experience that meant a great deal to Karla — and to all of us.

Later that month, we were in the day clinic for chemo when Dr. Jubran told Karla she would be beginning her next round on June 29, which also happened to be Karla's fifteenth birthday.

"I am not doing chemo on my birthday," Karla said emphatically. I was taken aback, but Dr. Jubran simply said, "Okay, no chemo on your birthday." And that was that. Instead, Karla decided to go away for a week to Lake Havasu to celebrate her birthday with her dad, his new girlfriend, Colleen, and Courtney. It was the first time I'd been apart from Karla on her birthday, but it gave Karla an opportunity to spend time with her dad's girlfriend, to whom she felt connected almost immediately from their first meeting in the hospital. (What Karla could control, she certainly did!)

Karla's trip with Rick was perfect timing, too, since her room was being renovated and was scheduled for completion by the time she returned home. The renovation was another one of those unexpected acts of generosity offered by strangers. The owners of an interior design company that was working in the home of Karla's friend, Courtney, met Karla when she was visiting one day, and after hearing her story, called the following day and simply said, "We have to do something for Karla."

Soon after, a team from Patrick Interiors started work on her surprise "room makeover." They came in and painted, created a built-in computer desk/vanity/display case, installed wood flooring, closet organizers, and brought in new furniture, pictures for her walls, and bedding. They even gave her a flat-screen TV and mini-refrigerator. During the month-long renovation, Karla moved into the downstairs playroom and never even peeked. She had tremendous willpower — for a fifteen-year-old girl! And when it was all over, she wound up with a room that was the envy of all of her friends.

～

Learned Wisdom

If you find yourself experiencing a rare moment of normalcy, don't feel guilty; soak it up and enjoy it, and give yourself the gift of not worrying about tomorrow.

Karla enjoying Los Angeles from a different view

Chapter 14

Laugh as much as you breathe and love
as long as you live.
— Anonymous

KARLA HAD FEW COMPLICATIONS from the ongoing chemo and was gaining strength every day. We anxiously awaited the results of her next MRI on July 19.

Email Update #10

July 20, 2005

Remarkable - Remarkable - Remarkable
We have some wonderful news to share. Tuesday, Karla under-
went an MRI to determine how well her tumor is respond-
ing to treatment since her last scan in April. We are excited
to inform everyone that the results are outstanding. Karla's
tumor is continuing to shrink at an amazing rate. Her doc-
tors at Children's Hospital Los Angeles are astonished at the
results. God is answering our prayers.
Karla's doctor stated that the results of the MRI are absolutely
"remarkable," and that the results are better than they could
have ever imagined back in January. When asked if there was

one single element of her treatment that was most success-
ful, the doctor had no clear explanation. He said, "I don't
know what it is, but I do know that your family has had a lot
of prayer, medicine, and the support of family and friends.
Our family sends a sincere thank-you to each and all of you.
We thank God for this wonderful news and ask for your con-
tinued prayers for Karla's healing as we travel on this journey.
Love to all,
Karla's family

With this incredible news came even more opportunities for adventure that summer. One of our favorites was a helicopter ride over Los Angeles. After months of making the forty-mile trek into L.A. for all of Karla's medical appointments and chemo and radiation treatments, we had come to dread the city. We began to associate it with only the hospital — and associate the hospital with cancer.

But then came a call one day from a friend who is a sergeant with the Los Angeles Police Department. Karla had baby-sat Derek's children, and he was devastated when he heard she was sick. He called in a favor from his lieutenant, and arranged for Karla and me to join in on a shift with the police department's helicopter, also known as the Air Support Division. We flew over Dodger Stadium, the Griffith Observatory, and Aaron Spelling's mansion — and got so close to the HOLLYWOOD sign we felt like we could almost touch it. We circled over a stakeout, watched the sunset — from a new angle! — saw the lights of the Santa Monica pier, and then waved to the folks eating dinner atop the tallest building in downtown L.A. Seeing the city lights from above was a sight I'll never forget.

Afterward, we had a "police escort" to Tommy's Burgers for a messy chiliburger that we ate on the hood of the police cruiser. Noticing the glances while we were in line for our food, Derek said loudly in his gruffest voice, "Listen you two, I'm going to feed you, then I want you out of this town for good!" Of course, we played along as everyone stared.

Not all of Karla's experiences that summer were fun, however. She was often sick and fatigued from chemo. She was also deeply aware of changes in her friendships. Longtime friends were moving in other directions, spending time with boyfriends, and having experiences outside the reality of Karla's world. When Karla wanted to just hang out at home and watch a movie, her friends wanted to go to parties. Some nights she would cry herself to sleep. Even so, Karla would talk about how lucky she was to have the friends she had and to be given opportunities to have adventures like she did that summer. Certainly, not all kids with cancer were given so much, she acknowledged.

One afternoon, Karla began having a "normal teenager attitude." She was downright rude to me. She wasn't on steroids, wasn't in the middle of a treatment, and had been doing "normal" teenage things with her friends. So when I told her, "Watch your tone of voice toward me" and her response was, "I don't want to," I slapped her mouth — not hard, but enough to let her know she couldn't talk to me that way. "Now go to your room until you have changed your attitude."

It was too late to tell her I was sorry that it had happened with her brothers watching. So once Karla slammed her door shut, I immediately called my mom, who's in her eighties, knowing that she would assure me I'd done the right thing. But she didn't. Her words were, "You can't touch that sweet thing — she's got cancer!" I felt awful but also at peace with myself for what I had done. Though I still regret this encounter, I still believe that, with her brothers watching her treat me like that, I did the right thing.

Karla's knack for always looking on the bright side gave the question "Why me?" an entirely new meaning. In fact, a psychologist at CHLA was so taken with Karla's ability to see the glass as half full that she asked that summer whether Karla would be willing to answer some questions on camera, in hopes that her perspective might help other therapists who work with children and teens. Of course, Karla agreed.

When I finally got up the nerve to play the video not long ago, I watched with pride as Karla, sitting cross-legged on a gurney while getting a chemo treatment, smiled brightly as she answered Dr. Robyn Westbook's questions about how she was coping with her illness.

"If you realize the good things instead of focusing on the bad, it's incredible how much it helps," she told Dr. Westbook. "Some people talk to therapists or go to support groups… staying positive is my own form of self-counseling, I guess."

During the interview, Karla spoke earnestly about how her friends, her family, and her faith helped her get through her roughest days.

"It's not like there was anything I could have done to control it or make it better or worse… and getting depressed doesn't help," she said. "You just have to be content with whatever you're given…. Once you accept it, it's ten times better. You just have to let it go."

Then she added: "I heard someone say it so perfectly: You don't ever wish to have this (cancer), but once you get through it, you wouldn't want to take it back. You learn so much, and it makes you realize what's really important."

Chapter 15

*It is the sweet, simple things of life which are
the real ones after all.*
— Laura Ingalls Wilder

I'LL NEVER FORGET THE DAY I checked my email and
found the note from a hospital social worker.

"Here are some resources you might find helpful," it read. It
was a list of websites for support groups both within and outside the hospital. Then came the offer that no parent wants her
child to receive: The social worker wrote that Karla "qualified"
to be the recipient of a gift from a wish-granting foundation.
It was as if the world were telling me that my child was going
to die — that she would be granted a "last wish" — and I wasn't
ready to accept that. My heart felt as though it had stopped — just
like it feels now as I write this.

About twenty years ago, when I was working as a flight atten-
dant, I encountered a young girl on a flight to Hawaii. With a
smile on her face, little Jennifer told me that she had leukemia
and that this trip to Hawaii with her mother was her "wish." I
was young and had never been touched by something so deeply.
I took special care of them during the flight, and later received
a lovely thank-you note from her with a few photos, including

one we had taken together during the flight. The pain I carry from that beautiful experience is that I never responded to her. I didn't know how. I never found out what happened to Jennifer, but I now understand firsthand what her mother was going through. And I know how a young child with cancer — a child you barely know — can touch your heart so deeply.

With some reluctance, Karla and I decided to attend a wish-granting meeting at the hospital. I remember sitting in the room feeling like I didn't want to be there. The representatives were very kind. They explained to the parents that the organization serves any child with a life-threatening illness — not just those who are terminal — so we should not see this as a "dying wish." They also encouraged the children at the meeting to "wish big" and go for their hearts' desire, so for the next several weeks the topic of many of Karla's conversations was: what did she want as her wish?

Karla was very excited when the time came for her personal interview. Unfortunately, it didn't go as anticipated. The foundation representatives assigned to Karla seemed detached and impersonal — far from the compassionate people we'd met at the first meeting. The questions included:

"What's your favorite movie?"

"What's your favorite candy?"

"Who is your favorite actor?"

And so on.

The two women seemed to grow impatient when Karla couldn't answer their questions fast enough, even though we hadn't known ahead of time that they would be asking about anything other than her wish.

Then came the question she had been waiting for: "So what's your wish?"

Since we were already planning a trip to New York once Karla was feeling better, she wanted to choose something different. After much thought — and with the encouragement to "wish

Above: Karla and her dads during her shopping spree

Left: Karla with Brandon getting his first limo ride

big" — Karla had decided she wanted, more than anything, to attend the MTV Video Music Awards with her friend Courtney. A few weeks later, someone from the organization called, discouraging her from her wish. They told us that the event was sometimes hot and uncomfortable for the kids, and that its organizers would likely give Karla no special consideration. "They don't treat the wish kids very well," we were told.

Karla was so disappointed, but finally she came up with another wish — shopping! Rick, Michael, and I tried to talk her out of it ("There must be a sight you want to see, an experience you want to have — something more meaningful than shopping!"), but she wouldn't budge. Like most fifteen-year-old girls, Karla loved shopping, and she especially loved the idea of returning to school in the fall with a new wardrobe.

During chemo, she and one of her favorite nurses, Alison, went online to research the best places to shop — somewhere she had never been — and they chose The Promenade in Santa Monica. Once again, however, the wish-granting folks encouraged Karla to change her wish: they advised that she would only have three hours there, so she might want to choose a mall that was easier to get to and easier to get around.

Of course, as her mother, I was the go-between during these conversations. I was beginning to feel an unexpected tension; I got the sense that they thought we were being overly demanding. I never wanted them — or anyone else — to think we weren't grateful for all of the wonderful gifts and experiences that were given to Karla; however, we were confused about why she was told, "Think big!" and then presented with so many restrictions. And, of course, each time she was told to change her wish, it was difficult to see her disappointment all over again.

Karla agreed to go to South Coast Plaza, another upscale mall in Southern California. Then she was told that neither her two closest friends nor Colleen, Rick's girlfriend, could join us — it was immediate family members only. Karla didn't want her little brothers joining her on a shopping trip, so she asked if her friends could come instead. The organization would not bend the rules. What started as a wish was now becoming a frustration. (After the shopping expedition, Karla's friends were waiting for her to have a "campout" in our backyard.)

The wish granters, who picked us up thirty minutes late, had allotted Karla $2,500 and told us that most of the stores would be expecting her and have special discounts to make her money go further. Unfortunately, that was not the case; the only person who knew she was coming was the makeup artist at Nordstrom, who gave Karla a makeover — and then tried to sell her makeup. On top of that, on the way to the mall, which is filled with designer stores, the organization representatives talked about another wish granting they had just come from where a little boy had asked for a Wal-Mart shopping spree. It was awkward, to say the least, but Karla's sense of humor — especially when she was with her dad — kept us all laughing.

Karla had a wonderful time shopping, and managed to spend $700 in the first clothing store she visited. While we are grateful for that day, I learned some hard lessons from that experience about how far a little compassion, flexibility, and a personal touch can go when it comes to supporting a sick child and making him or her feel special. These lessons would become more valuable to me than I could have ever realized at the time.

Learned Wisdom

A simple act of kindness can turn into your life-changing moment.

Above: Karla with members of her dance team in Fall 2004, before her diagnosis

Below: Karla back at school with her dance team and dance teacher, Danielle (far left) in Fall 2005

Chapter 16

You have touched more hearts
than you will ever know.
— My friend Cheryl Schmidt

THE MONTH BEFORE SCHOOL BEGAN, Karla was strong enough to join her dance team at camp in San Diego. She was able to keep up and felt good, but to no one's surprise, she came home exhausted. The day after she returned, she had a scheduled PET scan, another diagnostic imaging test, to give doctors more information about the change in the tumor's size and dictate her future therapy. The Monday after the test she was scheduled to begin her next round of daily chemotherapy.

Email Update #12
Aug. 19, 2005

I can't possibly put into words how happy I am to tell you the good news that we received last Monday (August 8th). After getting the results of my PET scan they learned that my tumor is mildly active, so I no longer have to get intravenous chemotherapy! This basically means that I get to have my life back... no more feeling sick all the time, no more extreme lack of energy, and no more daily trips to the hospital! It was probably the best news that I will ever hear.

I will, however, still have to take chemo in a pill form, but this dose is much lighter, has nowhere near the same side effects, and can be taken at home. These pills unfortunately are chronic (I will take them throughout my entire lifetime), but I think of it as being no different than a diabetic having to take insulin shots every day to keep healthy. As far as my hospital visits go, I will go only once a month to get my blood drawn to make sure that my blood counts are normal. Also, every 90 days, I will receive an MRI just to monitor the tumor and to make sure that it is not growing (which, of course, it's not going to!).

I have gone nearly four weeks now without my IV chemo, and I am definitely enjoying both my health and my freedom. I have been dancing, boating, playing soccer, and having fun with my friends. My prayer request is that God continues to show His power and ability to perform miracles. Even my doctors have admitted that my progress is undoubtedly the workings of both prayer and medicine combined. I also pray that my body's health remains the same and that my tumor does not and will not ever grow.

THANK YOU SO MUCH... MY FAMILY'S, FRIENDS' AND COMMUNITY'S SUPPORT HAS HELPED ME GET THROUGH THIS TOUGH JOURNEY!

All my love,
Karla

We heard from well-wishers everywhere — even people we didn't know:

Karla,
I am sure that you don't remember me, but I am the father of John. I met you at Lake Havasu where you, your girlfriend and the group of younger kids and I played games at the picnic table on our last evening there.

You gave me one of your bracelets, which I still have.
Kathy was nice enough to forward your email with the news
that you were no longer tied to the daily IV-administered
chemo. I am so happy for you and your family. You have been
in my prayers since our meeting, and although it's not the final
answer that I was praying for, it will rank as a close second.
If it's OK with you, I'll keep working on my original request.
You are truly an impressive young lady who will continue
to affect the lives of many people with your sparkling per-
sonality and a true inner strength and beauty that is most
unusual in any person, young or old.
With love and prayers,
Steve

When it was time to go back to school in the fall, we scheduled a meeting with the principal at Karla's high school to ensure
that she would receive the needed care and support during her
transition. Dr. Westbook from Children's Hospital Los Angeles
joined us. When we walked into the conference room, it was filled
to capacity with administrators, faculty, staff, counselors, and
nurses. The support was above and beyond what I had expected.

Even though Karla suffered from short-term memory loss,
she made it clear that she wanted no special privileges; in fact,
one of the reasons for the meeting was to make sure that everyone knew she wanted to be treated like everyone else. She didn't
want to jeopardize graduating on time or getting into the college
of her choice because of a lighter workload or a lenient grad-
ing system. The only thing I asked of her teachers was to let me
know if Karla exhibited any changes in personality or behavior.
We learned that just because circumstances beyond your control take away *some* of your choices it doesn't mean they have to
take away *all* of your choices.

Karla was so happy to be going back to school. She wrestled
with the decision of whether to wear a wig or just wear her "new"

hair in a short style. We wound up going to L.A. with her friends, Courtney and Kassey, to see about getting a new wig for school. At the wig shop, a talent scout told Karla how adorable she was with her short hair, and gave her a business card. The girls had a ball trying on some zany wigs, but in the end, Karla decided to stick with her "real" hair. She was relieved to be done with wearing wigs, and everyone at school commented on how great she looked with her short hair.

After the first week, she came home one day and said that the principal and the assistant principal had called her into the office to ask how she was doing. Even though soda had been removed from the campus vending machines, they asked, "Would you like a soda or some candy?" She declined the offer, but clearly was pleased that they were willing to break the rules for her. Though Karla insisted she wanted to be treated like everyone else, those special little considerations made her feel cared for.

Around the same time, during a hospital visit, we heard some exciting news: one of Karla's favorite bands, Maroon 5, would be having a private concert for the teenagers at the hospital. Not long after, the band's guitarist, James Valentine, offered private lessons on a weekly basis for a small group of teens. Karla had never demonstrated a desire to learn how to play the guitar, but when the hospital's psychologist asked if she was interested, Karla didn't hesitate. James gave Karla a guitar and, in the short time they had together, they developed a friendship. He gave her his email address and one day asked her, "Hey Karla, how come you never email me?" She told me later that she didn't want to take advantage of his kindness. That was so like Karla.

It may not have been on key or in rhythm, but some of the most beautiful sounds I've ever heard came from Karla's room, where she and her brothers sat strumming their guitars.

Email Update #13
October 21, 2005

The past few months have been great! Karla is back at school with a full schedule of classes. She is back to dancing with her dance team… a few weeks ago, she performed for the first time since January (it was so awesome to see her strength! Of course, I cried.) With lots of determination, she also is back practicing with her soccer team, Stampede. Her goal is to begin competitive play in January. She loves it! Her positive attitude shines so bright. We are so proud of her. Thank you to her dance and soccer coaches for your support.

During the past month, Karla has been suffering minor complications from pancreatitis. This has caused a delay in her chemo [pill] regimen. Treatment will not begin until doctors are comfortable that the healing process is working. This means she is currently on no medicine to stop that tumor. We are relying only on prayer. I ask all of you to continue to keep Karla in your prayers. I know our God is listening to all of them.

With love,
Ruthe

∼

Learned Wisdom

Just because a circumstance beyond your control has taken away some of your choices it doesn't mean it's taken away all of your choices.

Ryan and Karla at
deployment, March 2005

Karla and Cole waiting
for Ryan's return at
Edwards Air Force Base,
October 2005

Chapter 17

Never, never, never give up!
— Winston Churchill

WITH ALL THAT WAS HAPPENING in our lives that year, it was easy to lose sight of what was going on in the world around us. When the son of a friend from church was preparing to leave for Iraq, I asked if he would be willing to come over and meet with Karla before he left. This was in March 2005, when Karla was quite sick. Out of respect for her wishes, we had asked for no visitors, but when I told Karla that Ryan would be coming over before he left, she was thrilled.

During Ryan's visit, we sat on the floor of her bedroom — Karla and I, Ryan and his mom, Linda, Brandon, and Cole — and we prayed. Karla prayed for Ryan's safe return, and Ryan prayed for Karla's healing. After Ryan's deployment, he and Karla exchanged emails.

About six months later, in October, we were honored when Ryan's family asked us to be part of the group going to Edwards Air Force Base to welcome him home. Karla was looking and feeling so much better now; her smile lit up the hangar. We almost cheered watching them hug. Ryan then put down all his gear, reached into his left-sleeve pocket, and pulled out the blue

Amen bracelet that he had kept in his uniform the entire time.

Later that fall, Karla privately wrote a letter to the teen magazine *CosmoGirl*. Karla was always a good writer. As she got older, she talked of making it her career. When I read this letter, I was more convinced than ever that it would have been the right path for her. We found it on her computer months later; she had never submitted it.

I'm a Brain Cancer Survivor

Hi, CosmoGirl!
I'm 15 years old, and this past January I was faced with the unimaginable. I was a busy teenager with a 4.0 GPA and was actively involved in soccer and my school dance team. On January 7, 2005, I had to leave my school pep rally early to go for a CT scan for the unbearable headaches I had been having for a few months. After having an MRI to clarify their results, our greatest fears were confirmed — I had a cancerous, inoperable brain tumor called brainstem glioma. I was immediately admitted to the hospital, and within the next few days had surgery to place a tube, called a shunt, in my brain to relieve my excruciating headaches. I also had a Port-A-Cath (a device to make it easier to access your veins) inserted in my chest for the intravenous chemotherapy that I would be receiving.
I knew the possible outcomes of my horrible condition, yet I was not truly afraid. I am a girl of huge faith, and gave my illness completely to God. I believed strongly that God was using me to tell people of His ability to perform miracles, although I wasn't quite sure what exactly that miracle was going to be. Also, the outpouring of love from everyone around me was amazing. My whole room was full of 'get well' gifts from my friends, family, church, classmates, and community. I got boxfuls of cards from everywhere from Chino Hills to

Canada to Australia to Iraq (word of mouth had traveled far!). Blue bands were made (similar to the Lance Armstrong bands) that say 'Amen' on them, and over 10,000 were sold to help with my medical bills.

Despite all of the incredible love and comfort others gave me, I could not avoid the treatments I needed to save my life. For the next six weeks, every day, I not only received radiation to my brain, but intravenous chemo, chemo in a pill form, and steroids (not the ones that give you muscles or anything, ones that doctors use to reduce swelling). It was the hardest time of my life. I was constantly throwing up, had no appetite, and rarely had enough energy to get out of bed.

Also, I had to shave my long, blonde hair that I loved so much. I simply did not want to see large chunks of my hair on my pillow when I woke up in the morning, so I made the painful decision to take care of it myself. I hesitantly started to wear wigs, and after awhile, learned to accept my new 'accessory'. The steroids also had side effects of their own. My whole body bloated, especially my face. I went from a size 0 jeans to a size 5. A painful rash broke out on my whole body, again, especially on my face.

That same month happened to be Winter Formal at my school. Although I was getting a tutor at home due to my illness, my class nominated me for Winter Formal court. My friends encouraged me to go, so I built up strength to attend the dance. Despite a wig, a face twice the size of my usual, and a lot of makeup to cover-up my rash, I was able to forget my circumstances for a night, have fun with my friends, and win freshman Winter Formal princess.

Although that night was unforgettable, I still had to return to reality. I was taken off of steroids, and after all of the horrible side effects had ceased I thought that there would be few side effects to come. I was wrong. I was put in the hospital for almost a month, having pancreatitis, typhlitis, esophagitis, and gastritis, all painful stomach complications that banned all food and water. That meant that I had to be placed on IV feeds every night to replace the food and water that was taken away from me for over seven weeks.

Despite all of the terrible things that were going on, I hung on to hope. Getting a taste of fun and friends again at my winter formal allowed me to keep fighting. I did not let go of my faith and still believed strongly that it was all going to be okay in the end. After what seemed like years, it was time for my next MRI. I have to get anesthesia because I am very claustrophobic, so as I was coming out of it, all I heard the doctor say was 'It shrunk significantly!' My heart was relieved. All this horrible medicine was working. We were praising God that it was shrinking, but it did not mean that I was taken off the intravenous chemotherapy. For the next couple of months I remained extremely sick, losing over 20 pounds. The time for my third MRI was coming nearer, along with a new test, called a PET scan that determines how active my cancer cells are. I, once again, prayed for a miracle. My prayers were once again answered, this time in a huge way. My tumor had shrunk even more, so much that I no longer had to take the awful intravenous chemo. Also, the PET scan revealed that my cancer cells were mildly active, meaning that they produce at an extremely slow rate. I did, however, still have to take chemo pills, and this would continue throughout my lifetime. They do not make me anywhere near as sick as the IV chemo though, and my body will eventually get so used to them that they shouldn't affect me at all. Nobody can say, however, what amazing technology is to come. Who knows? Maybe someone will come up with a cure for cancer.

As for now, after about three months of completely being off of IV chemotherapy, I couldn't be happier. After missing six months of school, I was able to take on a full schedule of classes this past fall. I have been fully involved in my dance team again, and have begun to start practicing soccer. I have only known two other people with my condition: one passed away, and one has been struggling for life in the hospital for many months. I now know, because of what I am able to accomplish once again, what miracle God wanted me to pass on — the miracle of life. Thanks to my cancer, I now do not sweat the small things in life and live it to its fullest.

Above: Delivering "Komfort from Karla" baskets at the hospital

Left: Karla on her way to the Homecoming Dance

Chapter 18

*...faith is the assurance of things hoped for,
the conviction of things not seen.*
— Hebrews 11:1.

BY THE END OF OCTOBER, Karla's pancreatitis was gone and she was back on chemo pills. Even though she had not been having chemotherapy, her doctors told us the tumor wasn't growing — in fact a mass they had been watching had disappeared. The doctors were very pleased with her progress.

Karla's blood count, however, was still very low, making her susceptible to infections. It was decided that she should not return to school until her numbers rose. But we couldn't keep her away from the homecoming dance that fall. Helping Karla get ready for that dance was so, well, normal! There was the usual stress associated with finding the "perfect" dress — but we no longer had wigs, weight gain, or rashes to deal with. She went to the dance with a group of girlfriends, and they had a wonderful time. Karla even spent the night at a sleepover afterward.

Though Karla was still close with her circle of friends, we noticed that some weren't coming around as much anymore. I think Karla was growing tired of friends who only visited when she was feeling good and weren't willing to spend time with her when she wasn't. She was spending more time with Adam, whom she had met at church camp two summers earlier, and his girlfriend Melissa. Michael trusted Adam enough that he would even let Karla ride with him (it didn't hurt that he drove his parents' minivan!).

Just before Thanksgiving, Karla was invited to speak to the students at New Hope, a local Christian school where my boys attended preschool. Karla was always drawn to young children. During several of our trips to the hospital, she handed out baskets — filled with blankets, games, books, and more — to sick children. Some friends at our church had put the baskets together at Karla's request. They called them KOMFORT FROM KARLA baskets, and Karla loved delivering them. I wish those children could know how much their smiling faces meant to us.

At New Hope, Karla's presentation was to be about what she was thankful for. She asked me to join her onstage; she wasn't sure what she was going to say, and she wanted me to be there, just in case.

Karla was completely at ease with the children. She shared some information about her diagnosis, losing her hair, her weight gain and loss, having to stay out of school, and not being able to eat for a month. The children listened intently. Then she told them that she remembered how she used to look forward to Thanksgiving — but only because it meant that Christmas wasn't far off. But now, she said, the holiday had a new meaning for her. She appreciated all of the things in her life that she had taken for granted before — not the least of which was the ability to eat a huge Thanksgiving dinner!

A couple of months later, we received an email from one of the parents whose child had heard Karla speak:

When my daughter came home, she told me how strong and determined Karla was and how she looked up to her. My daughter has never spoken so highly of anyone in her life. Those few minutes with Karla made her realize that she was *placed on this Earth to change the lives of others. ... Since then she has done a walk for autism, raising over $150 by herself. She has collected goods to send to the military in Iraq. And she has just been a kinder child. I just wanted to thank you for raising such an inspiration to others.*

At the end of November, we were back at the hospital. Karla was having difficulty swallowing again. After another round of testing, doctors said everything looked fine; they couldn't figure out why she was having problems. I remember how happy Karla was when the doctor said they were removing her Port-A-Cath; it was a huge milestone because it was confirmation that she didn't need any more IV chemo. A week later, when Karla had the port removed, she was in such a good mood that we wrote our Christmas cards while we waited for her to be called into surgery.

Her blood count was up, too. She was back at school on an intermittent basis. Many days she was just too tired, but we chalked this up to her lingering fight with pancreatitis. Still, her spirits remained unshakeable.

December was filled with Christmas spirit, but also with more uncertainty. All of Karla's tests were coming back fine. The tumor, they told us after another CT scan, hadn't grown. But Karla was experiencing blurred vision and trouble with her balance. One morning she woke up and her radiant smile was lopsided. What was going on? We rushed her to the hospital. On the way, I called our pastor's wife, Carol, and expressed my fear. The hope that I had clung to for so long was wavering now.

"I don't feel God," I told her tearfully. "What does this all mean?"

"Today is a day of knowing, not feeling," she told me. I understood: I had to know that God was with me, even if I didn't feel His presence.

When we got to the hospital and they ran some tests, I was assured that the problems Karla was having weren't cause for alarm. "It's possible that part of the tumor is dying off," Dr. Jubran said, explaining that the changes in the tumor could be causing Karla's symptoms.

"Are you saying what we think you're saying?" I asked, incredulously.

"It's possible that it is dying off, and that is where the nerve is being affected," she elaborated. We took a moment to let it all sink in.

"You know where our faith is, and we totally trust your wisdom and all the medicine you are giving her," I told Dr. Jubran. "Knowing that all things are possible with God, we are going to leave with that hopeful news." We hugged and wished Dr. Jubran a merry Christmas, knowing we would be back for an MRI after the holidays.

This was another lesson we learned during our journey: You do your homework in the beginning, and find the doctors and facilities you believe are the best to treat your particular illness. Then, the key — at least for us — was to place our trust in those doctors. That doesn't mean we didn't ask questions or see ourselves as Karla's healthcare advocates, but we did not often second-guess our doctors' treatment plans or turn to the Internet to investigate every test that was ordered or prescription that was written.

Sometimes that was difficult, especially when well-meaning people — friends, acquaintances, even strangers — would ask questions about Karla's course of treatment.

"They're giving her *that?*"

"Why haven't they tried *this* on her?"

For some people, I believe that doing their own research and suggesting alternative treatments is, in fact, a source of therapy; it is empowering to see yourself as in charge of your own medical care, and I'm sure that some people have indeed improved their health by suggesting other courses of treatment, based on their independent research, to their doctors. When Karla was first diagnosed, before we began any radiation or chemotherapy, my husband did research her doctors and interviewed leading brain-tumor specialists from other hospitals, but we took greater comfort in knowing that we had found doctors whom we believed to be the best qualified to treat Karla. We put our trust and faith in their expertise — and I have never regretted that decision.

That weekend, with my heart filled with hope and yet uncertainty that I couldn't shake, I heard Pastor Scott say during his message at church something that I needed to hear: "When the facts end is when faith begins."

~

Learned Wisdom

Expect days when you will doubt your faith, and when they happen, find your strength in what you know, not what you feel at the moment.

Above: Karla, Brandon, and Cole Christmas 2005
Below: Karla and me, Christmas 2005

Chapter 19

Worry never robs tomorrow of its sorrow,
only saps today of its joy.
— Leo Buscaglia

"MOM, I WANT THIS TO BE THE BEST Christmas ever," Karla told me. "Not for materialistic stuff, but with memories."

Decorating the house at Christmastime with Karla, drinking hot apple cider, and holiday music playing in the background was a tradition. She was good at it; I relied on her opinion and creativity as we adorned the house and trimmed the tree, but this year we felt a special kind of joy. I wouldn't let myself get depressed, though I knew that the year ahead held many uncertainties. Even with the doctors' assurances, Karla's failing eyesight, poor balance, and crooked smile were worrisome signs I couldn't ignore. I couldn't help but wonder whether this was the last Christmas I would spend with my daughter, but I also knew that dwelling on the "what ifs" would rob me of these precious moments with her.

The season was filled with parties — and we hosted most of them! Over fifty relatives attended our annual family party, and we hosted our yearly mother-daughter tea with Karla's best friends and their moms. We also hosted a caroling party for our close friends, with a visit from Santa and a crafts table that Karla organized for the younger children. I'll admit that I tried talking Karla out of all the celebrations; after the past year, the last thing I felt up to was hosting duties, but she insisted we do them all. Now, when I look back, I realize what a gift those memories are. It truly was the best Christmas ever.

One day close to Christmas the phone rang. I answered to hear a young voice ask, "Is Karla there?"

"Yes, she is. May I tell her who's calling?"

"It's Christina."

It was to Christina's mother that I'd given my first Amen bracelet. Two days later, Christina, her mom, and her sister came to visit us at home. We shared stories, we laughed, and we prayed. Though Christina had difficulty walking, she glowed with heavenly spirit and with pride for what she had overcome. After they left, Karla and I discussed how bad we felt because of the challenges Christina was facing compared to how well Karla was doing.

I was planning a surprise for Christmas morning: I had heard that our pastor's golden retriever had just given birth to a litter, and, without even asking Michael, I decided that a puppy would be the perfect Christmas gift to the family — especially Karla. Though the kids had wanted a puppy after our beloved Samoyed died a year earlier, until now I just hadn't been able to consider getting a dog with all that was going on in our lives.

At Christmas, the puppies were still too young to leave their mother, so I took a photo of them and put it on our computer. On Christmas morning, after all the presents were opened, I told everyone I had one more gift, and led them to the computer screen. I'll never forget how excited they all were — and the smile on Karla's face. A few days later, we visited the puppies, and a few weeks after that, Michael and I took Karla (without the boys) and let her choose one. We named him "Karla's Bentley." He wasn't yet ready to leave his mother, but in the days that followed, the pastor's son, Andrew, snuck him over to see

Karla. I saw a spark between Karla and Andrew, and Bentley was the perfect "go-between." Bentley officially joined our family at the end of January, and was (and still is) a constant source of joy — and commotion!

On Friday, January 6, 2006, we were celebrating Brandon's birthday with a trip to Treyarch/ActiVision, the video game manufacturer, in Santa Monica. Brandon brought some friends for the private tour, and Karla reluctantly joined us. She had been sleeping a lot lately and I was starting to get a bit worried. During the tour, she clung to my arm. Her balance was off and she was having terrible double vision. At one point, she asked to go back to the car and take a nap, but I insisted she stay with us. In the group photo we took that day, her smile hid how awful she must have felt.

I called the hospital when we got home, but Dr. Jubran wasn't on call. Instead of spending all night in the ER and the weekend in the hospital, Karla and I decided we would wait until Monday. She stayed in bed a lot that weekend, but she didn't have a fever, so I wasn't overly concerned.

Early Monday morning, I awoke to Karla at my bedside.

"Mom, wake up," she said frantically. "My face — something is wrong with my face." Startled, I jumped out of bed and turned on the light. The left side of her face had fallen. I felt panicked, but I tried not to let it show.

As we prepared to drive to the hospital, I called to speak to Barbara, the nurse in charge. I felt even more distraught when she told me to pack our bags and plan on staying for a few days.

As I got Brandon ready for school and Cole ready for preschool, I looked downstairs and was reminded of all of the Christmas decorations that had been gathered but not packed up yet. I'm not sure why — I suppose the stress of the situation had gotten to me — but I couldn't handle the idea of leaving for a few days without first putting away the Christmas decorations. I called my friends Kathi and Cheryl and asked if they would come over as soon as they could to help put the decorations away before we left for the hospital. As Cheryl and I worked feverishly, Kathi went upstairs to help Karla get packed. Just as we finished, there at the top of the staircase was Karla, with the biggest smile on her face. "I'm ready to go now," she announced. We all were amazed at her ability to smile — no matter what challenges she faced.

When we got to the hospital and met with Dr. Jubran, Karla told her with a laugh that she couldn't stay long. "I need to get out of here so I can take driving lessons."

Dr. Jubran laughed and said, "Maybe we should work on clearing up your vision first and then we'll talk about driving." She admitted Karla for what she called a "tune-up," and an MRI was scheduled for Wednesday.

Learned Wisdom

Laughter shared with a loved one, no matter what the circumstances, is never inappropriate. The fact that something terrible is happening doesn't mean you shouldn't find humor in the moment.

Chapter 20

But things just get so crazy, living life gets
hard to do,
And I would gladly hit the road, get up and
go if I knew
That someday it would bring me back to you.
— "Sunday Morning," Maroon 5

I WAS ALWAYS AT KARLA'S SIDE just before her MRI and CT scans. I would hold her hand in mine and whisper in her ear, "Do you feel God?" and she would always silently reply yes with a nod. Then, as the anesthesia was being pushed through the needle, I would say softly, "With God, all things are possible." Each time, a tear would run down Karla's cheek and then she would be out, sleeping peacefully. I'd gently wipe the tear from her face, kiss her cheek, and leave the room, joining family and friends waiting outside.

But this MRI was different.

As they began administering the medication, Karla became combative, kicking and screaming. We had to hold her down until she was sedated. She was asleep before I had the chance to whisper in her ear. Instead of wiping away a single tear, I simply kissed Karla's tear-streaked face, tasting the salty tears. I walked out and waited. Rick and Courtney, and Courtney's mom, Jacque, were there, too. It was awful to see Karla go through that, but I truly wasn't worried about the results. It wasn't that I was in denial, but that I had learned to live in the moment. I chose to have hope. It wasn't until later that it became clear why Karla hadn't wanted to have that MRI. Somehow, she must have known.

The test took longer than usual; afterward, we wheeled Karla back to her hospital room and got her into bed. I was on my way to the restroom when I saw the doctor and several other people getting off the elevator and heading toward her room. That's when it hit me: They had bad news. I felt my knees buckle, but I caught myself and thought, *I can handle this.* I saw arms reach out to hug me — I didn't even register whose they were — and the doctor suggested we find a private place to talk.

"Anything you have to say to me you can say in front of Karla," I said firmly. "The one thing I won't allow you or anyone to do is to give Karla a timeline. Only God will give her that." They agreed.

Dr. Jubran sat at Karla's bedside and explained to her that the tumor had grown. It was now larger than when she was first diagnosed a year earlier. A tear ran down Karla's face. I felt numb, but I didn't cry until later. I'll never forget watching the nurse pat Dr. Jubran on the back as she talked to us — even the doctor needed comforting.

While I knew this day could come at any time, the reality felt like running into a brick wall. I went out to the hall to phone Michael, who was on a business trip and due home the following day. I insisted that he continue his trip; after all, there was nothing any of us could do. He turned around halfway to his destination and was home by midnight.

Half an hour after we got the news, James Valentine stopped by to visit Karla, since she had missed her guitar lesson that day. Our red, swollen eyes and the somberness of the room told him all he needed to know. Still, he sat down and opened his laptop so Karla could listen to what the band was working on. Then he grabbed her guitar and starting playing and singing one of his band's hits, "Sunday Morning." Before long, we were all gathered around singing, laughing, and somehow displacing the pain. Watching how much Karla was enjoying herself, I joined in, reluctantly. Other patients and nurses pulled up chairs in the hallway outside the room to listen. Just then, Karla's food arrived. It was the first time in three days that Karla was able to eat, and she wasn't going to wait just because she was getting a private concert from one of the biggest rock stars of the year. "Sorry, but I'm eatin'!" Karla said. We all laughed.

After James left, so did Courtney and Jacque. Karla's dad was out of the room, making calls. It was our first time alone since we'd gotten the news. I climbed into bed with Karla, but as soon as I started to talk, Karla abruptly said, "Mom, I don't want to talk to you." I felt hurt, but I also knew I needed to respect her space.

Karla loved her guitar lessons with
James Valentine of Maroon 5.

Within minutes, Lexie, a patient with whom Karla had become friends, came to visit, as did three of my dearest friends, Kathi, Lisa, and Lisa, who had been called with the news. It wasn't long before Karla and Lexie were laughing and calling "room service" for a late-night snack.

It was close to midnight when I asked my friends to drive me home. I hadn't told anyone what Karla had said to me, but her dad was there to spend the night. I felt that Karla and I needed some time apart — and I needed to be home. Michael was in bed when I got there, and he held me until I could sleep.

Chapter 21

Let not your heart be troubled,
neither let it be afraid.
— John 14:27

THE NEXT DAY, Michael and I returned to the hospital to bring Karla home. She was still asleep when the nurse told me that someone from Hospice would be contacting us. I was still numb from the night before and I wasn't ready to hear that word, "Hospice," a word we associate with the elderly — and impending death. The nurse explained that Karla would soon lose all mobility, as well as her ability to eat or communicate. I wanted her to stop. I wanted to scream and throw up at the same time. I told myself that God was in control — no matter what the doctors and nurses predicted. I was reminded of what Karla once told me: "If it's not happening and it's not a fact, then I don't want to talk about it." It was exactly what I wanted to tell the nurse, yet I knew I needed to listen to what she was saying.

There was more: Karla could take part in an experimental chemo trial. The department's head nurse told us in no uncertain terms that this would not cure Karla. It could give us a little more time with her, and its results could be helpful to researchers. We wouldn't be doing it for Karla, she explained, but for others down the road. If she said yes, it meant back on weekly chemo, on a strict diet to prevent the return of her pancreatitis, weekly weigh-ins — it pretty much meant that she would be on it until her body was too weak to take any more. Before we left the hospital, Rick, Michael, and I decided that we would leave this decision up to Karla.

We held back our tears as we said our good-byes to the nurses. One of Karla's favorite nurses, Sona, took me aside and, her eyes welling with tears, asked me, "How do you have so much faith?" I don't remember what I told her, but I do remember that it felt good to feel that God was working through me.

Karla and some of her favorite nurses in February 2005 (above) and November 2005 (below)

We checked out, and I anticipated a very long, quiet ride home. To my surprise, Karla wanted us to stop and pick up food before we even got on the freeway. She ate and talked to Michael all the way home. I don't remember any of that conversation; I just watched the world going by around me.

We asked our friends to put the word out that we'd prefer no visitors that night. We were emotionally exhausted and wanted to be able to shower and get into bed. Karla and I still hadn't talked about the MRI results. I just kissed her and the boys goodnight and fell into bed. I think sleep came while I was still praying.

It was midnight when Karla woke me with a whisper, "Mom, I'm hungry. Take me downstairs." Exhausted, I pulled myself out of bed; Karla was too unsteady on her feet to walk downstairs alone. As we walked, she laughed, as usual, at her wobbliness. I admired her ability to laugh at herself even at the most challenging times. And somehow, I managed to laugh, too.

Karla said she had just spent an hour crying on the phone with her friend Adam, discussing with him the decision she had to make about whether to participate in the chemo trial. By this time, Adam had taken on the role of a big brother; she trusted him and knew he would offer good advice. As it turned out, he told me later, Karla was the one with the answers that night.

"Karla told me that if she went back on chemotherapy and got healed, then people wouldn't know if it was the chemotherapy or if it was God healing her. But if she didn't go back on chemotherapy and got healed, then everyone would know it was a miracle," Adam said.

"She said she wasn't scared of dying — God is bigger than that. She said, 'I'm more scared about leaving the people I love, and my brothers still need me.'"

"It's easy to say you have faith," Adam said, "but Karla was really living it."

When Karla and I made our way downstairs, she sat down at the kitchen table. "Sit with me," she said. "I'm ready to talk now."

I sat at the table and watched her every move as she got out the bowl, the milk, the spoon, and the box of Rice Krispies. She ate and we talked.

"I don't know what I'm going to do," Karla said calmly. Dr. Jubran had told Karla that whatever choice she made about the chemo trial, it would be the "perfect" one. Karla and I both found great comfort in those words.

"This is your decision," I told her. "No matter what it is, both of your dads and I will support you one hundred percent." I told her we would provide whatever information or research she asked for. I warned her, though, that once she had made her decision, she shouldn't share it with anyone. Not even me. I didn't want her to be swayed.

"It's like a bride at the altar. The church is full, the gifts have all been sent, money has been spent, and your parents are looking on proudly — how can you turn and run?" I told her. "I want to give you the gift of changing your mind at the very last second, so until you give Dr. Jubran your answer, don't tell anyone."

Karla smiled.

"I'm leaning toward no more chemo," she said bluntly, pouring a second bowl of cereal. I did not respond. "If they can't give me facts about this trial, then I would rather just give it to God. He gives promises."

I felt pride and comfort in her words, but I didn't let on. "It is completely your choice," I repeated.

I never questioned her decision — not even for a moment.

"Mom, peel me a tangerine." As I did, Karla asked me the toughest question I've ever been asked as a mother.

"There was something I forgot to ask Dr. Jubran," Karla began. "If I don't do any more chemo and the tumor keeps growing, how long do I have to live?" My heart sunk. I didn't know what to tell her. Though the doctors had told us she could live one to three years, that had been at the time of diagnosis one year earlier and before all of the medical intervention.

"I don't know. I never asked," I said. "But I will if you want me to."

"Yeah, I do."

"You know, Karla, you should never ask a question that you really don't want the answer to," I said, unsure of whether it was the right advice to give.

Then, with an unexpected lightness and humor in her voice, she responded, "You're right. Don't ask."

"Are you sure?"

"Yeah."

Somehow, we both began to laugh. I'm not sure why, but it didn't matter.

"Peel me another tangerine?" she asked. I thought our conversation was over, but then Karla became quiet again. The conversation wasn't over for her.

"Mom, I don't see my purpose anymore," she said quietly. I had never heard such a lack of hope from her.

"Karla, your purpose is as clear as day," I told her earnestly. "You have inspired so many people with your faith and courage." We just sat there together in silence.

When she finished her tangerine, we agreed we needed to get some sleep. We giggled at Karla's clumsiness on our way back upstairs. I tucked her in with a kiss and a long hug. I remember smelling her, taking it in, trying to memorize that beautiful scent.

Learned Wisdom

When your worst fear stares you in the face, don't turn away; if you can find the courage to look it in the eye, you've accepted God's great gift of strength.

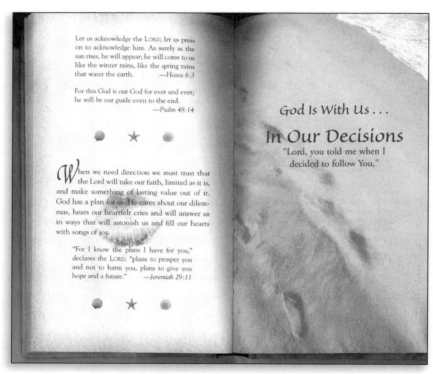

Let us acknowledge the LORD; let us press on to acknowledge him. As surely as the sun rises, he will appear; he will come to us like the winter rains, like the spring rains that water the earth. —Hosea 6:3

For this God is our God for ever and ever; he will be our guide even to the end. —Psalm 48:14

When we need direction we must trust that the Lord will take our faith, limited as it is, and make something of lasting value out of it. God has a plan for us. He cares about our dilemmas, hears our heartfelt cries and will answer us in ways that will astonish us and fill our hearts with songs of joy.

"For I know the plans I have for you," declares the LORD, "plans to prosper you and not to harm you, plans to give you hope and a future." —Jeremiah 29:11

God Is With Us . . .

In Our Decisions

"Lord, you told me when I decided to follow You,"

Nikki kissed the page with a resounding smack, and we all felt the joy and assurance of it.

Chapter 22

*Thanks for showing me what true faith
and pure trust look like.*
— My friend Nikki Stuart

A WEEK LATER, ON JANUARY 18, 2006, Karla had an appointment to give Dr. Jubran her decision. She and I agreed at the last minute that we wanted our friend Nikki to join us. Since Nikki's bout with breast cancer, the three of us — but especially Karla and Nikki — had formed a strong bond. While Nikki was doing well, I felt that it was important for her to see Karla at peace with her decision, regardless of what it was.

An hour after we called, we picked Nikki up for the trip to the hospital. We laughed all the way there. Before we knew it, the hospital was in sight.

"Hurry, Nikki — get out our prayer book and read us the perfect prayer for this appointment," I said excitedly. She flipped through the pages and picked one at random.

"'For I know the plans I have for you,' declares the Lord, 'plans to prosper you and not to harm you, plans to give you hope and a future.'"

It was the perfect prayer. Nikki kissed the page enthusiastically. "Now everyone will know it was me who read the prayer," she laughed.

Her lipstick print on the page serves as a beautiful reminder of that day.

As we approached the hospital elevator, we saw one of the top brain cancer specialists at CHLA. Throughout our journey, he had always seemed indifferent, even dismissive, when we would see him, as though Karla's type of brain tumor wasn't of particular interest to his research. But I suspect he had more interest in us than we knew at the time. There he was, holding the elevator for us. He greeted us as we got on.

"Hello, doctor," I said. "This is — " I began, ready to introduce Karla.

"I know who you are," he answered with a smile, turning to Karla. "I understand you have a big decision to make today."

That's why he was suddenly interested in her, I thought. He must be somehow involved in the chemo trial. Only now did we serve a purpose for his research.

"Yes, I do," Karla answered confidently. She had no intention of sharing her decision with him. She, too, must have picked up on his seemingly sudden interest in her case, only now, she was the one in control. Smiling, we got off the elevator.

We were led to an exam room, where we met with Dr. Jubran and Dr. Westbrook. She asked whether Karla had made her decision. Without hesitation and with a smile on her face, Karla pronounced confidently, "No more chemo!"

Dr. Jubran never tried to change Karla's mind, and neither did we. I could not have been more proud of my daughter.

Dr. Jubran halted all treatment and recommended some herbal medicines and heavy doses of green tea to help relieve some of the symptoms that were keeping Karla from attending school. When we left that day, there were no follow-up appointments or MRIs scheduled.

Though I was at peace with Karla's decision, I remember looking around the hospital corridors as I grabbed a cup of coffee from the coffee cart and we prepared to leave. At that moment, I realized I might never be back there.

~

Learned Wisdom

Building trust with your kids means following through on what you agree to do.

Above: Lexie, Karla, and Cole on the set of
"That's So Raven," January 19th

Below: Karla and Melissa before going to the
Supercross luncheon, January 20th

Chapter 23

Without faith, nothing is possible.
With it, nothing is impossible.
— Mary McLeod Bethune

DESPITE KARLA'S FAILING EYESIGHT and faltering balance, the following week was packed with activities. It wasn't planned; they were all last-minute invitations — and Karla always wanted to accept. Lexie invited her to go on a trip to the set of *That's So Raven,* and they got to meet its star, Raven-Symoné. Karla went bowling with friends (Melissa carried Karla on her back so she could throw the ball down the lane!) In fact, Melissa had become such a constant companion to Karla as she helped her keep her balance that we nicknamed her "walking stick."

There was a big Supercross race coming up, and Rick's girlfriend, Colleen, invited us to a Women's Auxiliary Supercross luncheon the day before the race. Colleen asked if I would give the opening prayer; I was touched, and it felt right. Though Karla had a great time that day — our friends had come beforehand to do her hair and nails — she told me afterward how upsetting it was to need so much help to get ready.

The next day, we went with some friends to the race and saw Rick, who was working there. On that day, I remember my heart breaking as we sat in the stands for the final few laps, and, as everyone stood cheering, Karla clung to my arm and asked, "Who's winning, Mom?" Though she was sharing our excitement, I realized that Karla's vision had become so poor that she could barely see.

That same week Karla asked to go to the hospital so that she could sit in on her scheduled guitar lesson with James. She wasn't able to hold her guitar, but she wanted to see him. They talked about how Karla's dad had a friend, Lois, who was arranging to get her and Melissa on the red carpet at the Grammy Awards on February 8, about two weeks away. Of course, James promised to look for her there.

Karla even received a package from Rick's friend, with a sparkling bronze dress to wear to the awards show. That beautiful dress hung in Karla's room for all to see when they came to visit. I know that I was there when she tried it on, but to this day I can't remember seeing her in it — my mind won't let me.

A few days later, I needed to go to the market, so I left Brandon with Karla for a few minutes. While I was gone, the doorbell rang; it was Rob Clements, the principal of Brandon and Cole's elementary school. Even though he had never been Karla's principal, Mr. Clements had been a huge support throughout our journey.

Karla, whose balance and vision had become progressively worse, had not been downstairs in several days, but when she heard that "Mr. C" had come to see her, she managed to walk downstairs, swaying side to side, to say hello. When Mr. Clements told me the story later, with tears in his eyes, I almost didn't believe him.

Not long after his visit, I had an idea: Over the past year, we had heard from hundreds of people, telling us how Karla's journey had affected their lives. They may have heard about her only from a friend, or read the account in the newspaper, but somehow Karla's story and the way she was handling her challenges made them reflect on their own mortality, on the way they cared for those around them, on their relationships with God, on their attitudes about life. And though Karla had received countless cards, letters, and emails, most of these touching stories were in passing, mentioned to us in conversation, through a friend, or relayed in church. Wouldn't it be great if Karla could hear all these stories? If she could read, in black-and-white, about the impact she had had on her community and beyond?

So, on January 24, I emailed the following to those who had signed up to receive our church email updates:

Greetings!

This past week, Karla and our family have enjoyed many visitors with so much love to share. We are also aware that there are so many of you who don't really know what to say or are asking us about our needs. Our needs are always for prayers of healing and God's peace through it all!

As far as what to say... well, my mind has been working overtime. Just because Karla has decided not to go with the "never been tried chemo" certainly doesn't mean that she is giving up! In fact, she has more hope and faith than she has ever had. But I will share that her spirits have been a bit down because of her recent physical challenges.

So I was thinking... maybe we could all (family, friends, community members... even those who have never met Karla) surprise her with a gift?

So many friends and family members have shared with me how their lives have been affected by Karla's incredible courage, strength, and amazing faith. I think that maybe it's time Karla heard these stories for herself. Do you think you could give Karla that gift?

If you know Karla, you know that she doesn't like being the center of attention, and if she knew I was doing this, I'd be in big trouble. But I have such confidence in the incredible

healing power that words can have, and I know what an
encouragement that this will be to Karla, that I want to step
out in faith and invite you to touch Karla's life with the gift
of your stories.
I want to invite you to be a part of this gift for Karla. Take
a minute to jot a couple sentences, a few paragraphs, or an
entire page to let Karla know about you and what her jour-
ney so far has done for you!
How has your life been touched by Karla's journey?

I asked everyone to email their answers to our church so that
they could be compiled and shared with Karla. It wasn't long
before the answers started pouring in. In fact, Mr. C's was one
of the first:

I would like to tell you about the 1,100 lives that have been
touched by Karla's story. Our character education program
this year focuses on how we cannot change the things we do
not control, but we can (and often should) control how we
respond. Karla's 'response' to her circumstances was used
as a moving and effective example during our first trimester
character education assemblies, which promoted the ABCs
of Character: Attitude is everything, Believe in yourself, and
Care about others. Her positive attitude under stressful cir-
cumstances, her belief in who she is through God, and her
ability to worry about others and their well-being while her
own being wasn't well, has served (and continues to serve)
as an awesome example of courage, leadership, and faith to
the 1,100 students who attend Wickman Elementary School.

A few days later, there was the email from Ryan, the soldier in
Iraq who had made such an impression on Karla:

I'll never forget that the last place that I went before head-
ing to Iraq was to visit with you and your family. Seeing your
strength and courage in the face of such adversity inspired
me and gave me strength during my deployment. ... I know
that people tell you all the time how amazing you are. But
you truly are! Don't let the fact that so many people tell you
that diminish the truth. When we were hanging out at your
house that time you made me laugh so hard. You have such
a great sense of humor and you are truly a fun person to be
around. Thank you for being you!

We received hundreds more notes and emails from close
friends, family members, acquaintances, and complete strangers. The ones that touched me most, I think, were the ones written by children and teenagers:

i miss you since the last time i saw you. not seeing that beau-
tiful smile of yours really just has a way of making my day
gloomy... i'm telling you, karla, everyone in this world loves
you so much it's incredible. even the people who don't know
you are totally moved by you because you are the most awe-
some girl in the world. ...everyone that has ever known you
is truly blessed. especially me.
— Christine

That Sunday, after I got ready for bed, I heard Katie Couric
interviewing the mother of Laci Peterson, the twenty-seven-
year-old California woman whose husband had murdered her
a few years earlier. Sharon Rocha had just written a book about
her daughter. Exhausted, I sat on the edge of my bed and listened intently to the interview, in awe of the woman's peaceful,
articulate demeanor.

Then I heard her laugh.

How could this woman laugh, I thought, after what she had

been through? My daughter had not been ripped away from me as hers was; over the past year, I had been able to have some of the most wonderful moments that a mother could hope to have with her child.

So when I heard Laci Peterson's mother laugh, it gave me hope that one day I might be able to laugh again. And at that moment I knew it was my duty to inspire others just as I had been inspired.

～

Learned Wisdom

Learning to let go isn't about accepting loss, it's about letting the person you love live life to the fullest, even when it means sharing them with others.

Chapter 24

To live in this world you must
be able to do three things:
to love what is mortal; to hold it against your bones
knowing your life depends on it; and, when the time
comes to let it go, to let it go.

— Mary Oliver, Pulitzer Prize-winning
author of "American Primitive"

ON MONDAY, JANUARY 30, Karla's high school dance teacher, Danielle, called and asked if she could visit. Karla had not had any visitors in several days. She had been on massive doses of steroids as a last-ditch attempt to relieve the swelling in her brain. She had complete double vision and relied on us for everything, even to sit up in bed.

When I explained to Danielle that Karla was not up to seeing visitors, she asked if she could come anyway to discuss the upcoming Dance of Hope, which, this year, would benefit another Chino Hills High student suffering from a life-threatening illness.

When Karla asked who had called, I told her that Danielle was coming over but did not expect to see her. It was important for me to show Karla that I respected her wishes. When she was first diagnosed, I expected Karla to see everyone who stopped by, whether or not she was feeling up to it. While it was Karla's nature to be outgoing and gracious, sometimes she wasn't up to seeing visitors, and I failed to respect her feelings during those early weeks. Eventually, we came up with a "secret word" that she would say when she wanted visitors to leave. It would be my signal to politely ask them to leave so that Karla could get some rest.

Now that Karla was on heavy doses of steroids, I was even more protective. The drugs were, once again, causing personality changes and irrational behavior. They made her so ravenous that she would constantly demand food, but I had been instructed to limit the amount she ate.

When she was on steroids, Karla was sometimes, well, not Karla. Before taking the pills, she would often apologize — in advance.

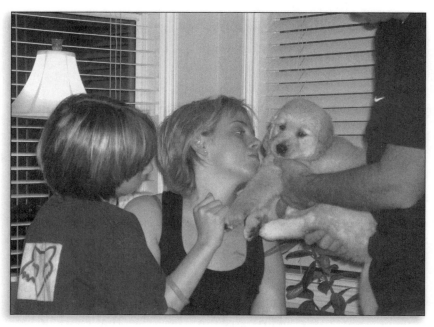

Karla with Brandon and Bentley,
our adorable new family addition

"I'm sorry, Mom, for anything I might say or do while I'm on these," she'd say. And I'd ask her forgiveness, in advance, for having to scold her if she got out of control. I still wrestle with the knowledge that I had to chastise my daughter when she was so ill.

That week, when I asked her if she wanted to see people — telling her that she didn't have to talk to them if she didn't feel up to it — she responded weakly, "It hurts just to smile, Mom." I was reminded how my daughter must be suffering — and that, especially now, I owed it to her to protect her privacy.

I told Karla that Danielle and I would be discussing the Dance of Hope. Though I had agreed previously to be on the planning committee, things were different now; Karla depended on me for assistance with almost everything. She could not walk on her own. I would use her wheelchair to take her from her bedroom to the bathroom. I blow-dried her hair, put lotion on her beautiful face, got her toothbrush ready, and helped her dress. I told Karla that I was going to let Danielle know that I couldn't help with the event because I needed to be there for her completely.

"No!" Karla exclaimed, surprising me. "You have to make that dance work, Mom. Promise me that you will make that dance work."

"Okay," I said, not knowing at the time how I would be able to take on this responsibility. This was the second of only two promises Karla would ask of me.

Karla asked to see Danielle when she arrived. It was a brief but powerful visit, and I am reminded of it each year when I get onstage to welcome the audience to the Dance of Hope. I am so proud to help carry out this annual event — and it is such an honor to carry out Karla's wish to help others who are going through tough times.

Two days later, Marianne, the local newspaper reporter, asked if she could come over to do a follow-up article.

"What is there to talk about?" Karla asked me. But she agreed to the interview.

Marianne conducted the interview at Karla's bedside, but Karla couldn't concentrate on the interview — she wanted a burger from In-N-Out! Marianne actually had to stop the interview and write down Karla's order on her notepad. She gave it to my sister, Ginny, who had come to help out. It was only then that Karla could concentrate on the interview. Afterward, for the first time in days, Karla said she felt up to coming downstairs to eat. I helped her down the stairs, and she sat in her wheelchair by the fireplace and played with Bentley, our new puppy.

That night, however, she felt miserable, and all she could do was cry. I felt helpless. In just a few short hours, Karla's condition had deteriorated so rapidly that she could no longer feed herself. Melissa came over and calmed her down and fed her a bowl of soup. That night, Karla fell out of bed crying and would not allow me to pick her up off the floor. I put a pillow under her head and covered her with a blanket to keep her warm.

Early the following morning, while it was still dark, I went into her room and found an open journal at her feet. The handwriting was hard to make out — I was stunned that she had been able to write at all, especially during the night, but there in her journal, my sweet daughter had written two prayers. They were short, sweet, and simple:

My dearest Heavenly Father,
Please show me your hopeful future.
Please help me to understand
My dearest Heavenly Father,
Please help me to understand the pain that I cannot take,
All the greatness that you have planned.

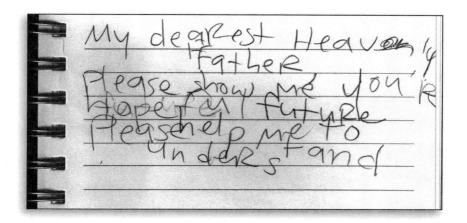

My dearest Heavenly
Father
Please show me your
Hopeful future
Please help me to
understand

My dearest Heavenly
Father,
Please help me to
understand,
the pain that i cannot
take,
all the greatness that
you have planned

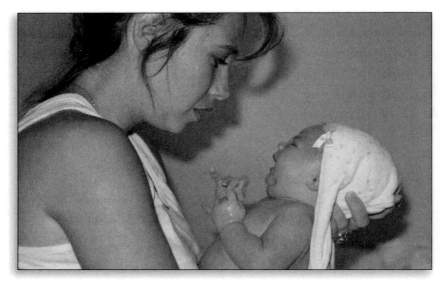

Karla and me after her very first bath, 1990

Chapter 25

Consider it pure joy, my brothers, whenever
you face trials of many kinds,
because you know that the testing of your
faith develops perseverance.
Perseverance must finish its work so that you
may be
mature and complete, not lacking anything.
—James 1:2

WHEN KARLA AWOKE THAT MORNING, she seemed different. She was quiet, and at peace. I still refused to accept the fact that she was dying, but I knew she was getting worse. Someone from Hospice had come, and though our initial meeting went well, the nurse they sent had a poor bedside manner and was of little help.

Fortunately, that same day, Dr. Jubran called and asked if she could come over. Karla was delighted to know that her doctor cared enough to make a personal visit. I was relieved to have the doctor come because Karla had fallen and hit her head in the bathroom that morning, and, for the first time since her diagnosis, she had a headache that would not go away.

When Dr. Jubran entered Karla's dimly lit room, Karla opened her eyes and smiled. Dr. Jubran reached down and put her hands on Karla's face, one on each cheek, looked into her eyes, and said, "I love you." I was so grateful for her compassion and love for my child. They had a brief conversation, and she examined Karla's head. She administered some morphine and waited until it took effect. She then injected some more, and soon Karla was asleep. Dr. Jubran will never know how much that visit meant to us.

In the middle of the night, Karla woke up vomiting from all the drugs. Her only words were, "No more medicine."

That afternoon, I decided to give Karla a bath. The shower was no longer an option; she couldn't even hold her head up. My sister helped me get her into our bathtub. Though I expected the Hospice nurse to help, she walked in and said, "If you need me I'll be downstairs doing paperwork."

I got into the bathtub with Karla to wash her fragile body. My daughter, who for the last several years had been so private about her body, had accepted that everything was now being done for her. She smiled gently as I looked into her beautiful blue eyes while I washed her. It reminded me of the first time I had bathed her as a newborn. It was as if nothing else existed in the world besides the two of us. But life was going on around us; we could hear Brandon and Cole jumping on the trampoline in the backyard.

My sister Ginny was there to help get Karla in and out of the tub. At the time, I was angry with the nurse for not helping, but if she had, I would have missed out on one of the tenderest moments I'd ever had with my daughter. Sometimes the most incredible opportunities for memories are right in front of us, and we don't see them. I'd like to think that I'm better able to recognize those moments today — because of Karla.

We got Karla dressed, and wheeled her back into her room. Though I had become very protective of Karla, and careful about whom I allowed upstairs to visit her, some friends and our pastors from church had stopped by and Karla wanted to see them. They gathered around her in prayer. She spoke only a few words, shared her warm smile, and accepted their tender words. It was evident to all there that Karla had completely surrendered to God — and that God was taking care of Karla.

Though I would discover later that most of our close friends were well aware that Karla was close to death, I truly did not know. I don't think I was in denial; I had heard months ago what her prognosis was. I just had come to believe with all my heart that Karla would live, and I would take on the role of the mother of a disabled child. Even at the end, I never lost hope, but when my friend Suzy, who is a pediatric ICU nurse, stopped by that day to check on Karla, I sat her down on the couch.

"Suzy, I have a question for you, and it's not based on my faith but on medical facts. Is Karla dying?"

"Based on medical fact and not on faith, I give her about two weeks," she responded solemnly.

I accepted the information, but I still clung to hope. As our pastor had said in church, "Faith begins when facts end."

Now, I was truly living on faith alone.

That night I slept with Karla. We laughed and talked more than we had in days.

"Mom, I'm sorry that I am causing you so much work," Karla told me. I held her close and we fell asleep. The next morning, my sister, with a smile on her face, told me that she had lain in bed in the room next to Karla's that night, and could hear us laughing and talking. The memories of that night still sustain me.

Saturday morning, the *Champion* newspaper ran Marianne's story. She had submitted it after deadline, so it wasn't supposed to appear in the paper until the following weekend, but after reading it, the editor had made an exception. It was titled "Hoping for a Miracle."

On Wednesday morning, lying on several pillows in her bed-room, Karla Asch-Rosen stated, somewhat matter-of-factly, 'The tumor is back and it's bigger than it was before.'
The 15-year-old Chino Hills resident, who has battled a brain tumor for the past year, said she wants the community to know she is struggling. 'I never knew it would be this hard....'

So many visitors stopped by that Saturday, including Courtney and her mom. The two girls snuggled together in bed, talking. Karla was alert, sitting up and even trying to eat a bit. I didn't allow many people up to see her. Her breathing was becoming more labored, and from outside her room you could hear the rhythmic sound of the oxygen machine we had recently gotten. Karla became weaker as the day went on, but at one point, when she heard us talking about ordering Italian food for all the people gathered downstairs, she interrupted: "I'll have spaghetti and a salad with ranch dressing, no onions or tomatoes." Karla had a way of lightening the most somber moments.

Later that day, I checked in on Karla again, leaned down to kiss her forehead, and asked how she was doing. I wasn't pre-pared for the answer.

"Mom, I'm ready to go be with God now," Karla said in com-plete peace.

Without thinking, I responded, "Then go, baby. Be with God now. It's okay. You've been the best daughter a mother could ever have. I will miss you so much, but I won't have to worry about you anymore."

Nothing can prepare you for that moment. I never imagined beforehand what I might say. The perfect words just came. With-out hesitation, I gave Karla my permission to go. And it really was okay.

As I gently kissed her and told that I would call her father, she said, "Mom, can you make me a smoothie?" Even feeling as I had never imagined I would feel, she made me laugh.

Immediately, I called Rick, and he and Colleen came over. There was only one other person I needed to call to come over: Nikki, who had bonded with Karla during her own courageous battle with breast cancer, needed to be there to see how at peace Karla was. She came as soon as she was called. I had never seen her so distraught. She told me later that, with all her being, she had believed Karla would live. She would never allow herself to believe there would be any other outcome.

Once Nikki had calmed down, we went upstairs. I could see Nikki was still shaking. I told her to sit down on the bed with Karla, which she did, reluctantly, not wanting to disturb her. I could see that Nikki needed some reassurance that Karla really was okay. I leaned down and said, clearly, "Karla, it's Mommy. Nikki's here, and she's very upset. I need you to tell her, are you scared?" Karla, eyes still closed, shook her head. "Are you in pain?" Again, no. "Are you ready to go?" She nodded.

With that, I left the two of them alone. Nikki told me later that she was stunned by what was happening and felt sick. She grasped Karla's hand and laid her head down on it, kissing it repeatedly.

"I have so much to tell you," Nikki said. "You've been such an angel to me. I'll never forget the hope you gave me. I couldn't have gotten through this without you." Nikki was startled when Karla, eyes still closed and with labored breath, said, "I'm so glad I could help."

Soon after, one of Karla's favorite nurses, Alison, showed up. I allowed her, too, up to Karla's room.

"They tell us not to get too close to patients, but who cares?" Alison said as she surprised me and leaped into bed with Karla, who was delighted to see her. By that time, Karla inexplicably had a burst of energy. When two of Karla's friends, Bianca and Adrianna, showed up, Karla had a smile for each of them and opened her arms wide. She was propped up in bed, laughing with the girls and Alison — they even painted her toes hot pink!

How could this be happening now? How could there be laughter coming from my daughter, who just told me she was ready to be with God? I tried to leave them alone as much as possible, even though I wanted every moment for myself. Their laughter gave me enormous peace (…it's about letting the ones you love live life to the fullest, even when it means sharing them with others.)

Downstairs, the house was filling with friends and family. The boys ran around as usual, with no idea what was happening. Then Dave, senior pastor at our church, and his wife, Carol, arrived to give Karla her last rites. We gathered around as he, already knowing the answer, asked Karla if she knew Jesus. She squeezed his hand tightly and nodded, and he smiled.

He read Psalm 23:

The Lord is my shepherd; I shall not want.
He makes me lie down in green pastures.
He leads me beside still waters.
He restores my soul.
He leads me in paths of righteousness
for his name's sake.

Even though I walk through the valley of the
shadow of death,
I will fear no evil,
for you are with me;
your rod and your staff,
they comfort me.

You prepare a table before me
in the presence of my enemies;
you anoint my head with oil;
my cup overflows.
Surely goodness and mercy shall follow me
all the days of my life,
and I shall dwell in the house of the Lord
forever.

I had the boys, one at a time, come in to say goodbye to their sissy. She hugged them and they exchanged their heartfelt "I love yous." I told them that when they woke up the next morning, their sister might be gone. I was that sure. Cole had entered the room first. And then the unexpected: "Brandon, come kiss Sissy good-bye, she's dying." I caught myself wanting to say "Don't say that, Cole," but then I realized that he was right. Karla was dying. Cole's peace and acceptance as he called to his brother was actually just what I needed.

I tried to leave Karla alone with Rick and Colleen as much as I could. I wanted to be at her side every moment, but I knew that they needed that time alone with her, too.

For the rest of the evening, with music playing softly in the background, family and friends surrounded Karla in her dimly lit room, reading to her the emails and gift letters people had written in response to my request. At one point, Karla told me I was reading too loud. We all laughed. It was her way of letting us know she was listening. This was not the way we had planned to give her these gifts, but the timing and the way we took turns reading them to her could not have been more perfect.

By midnight, almost everyone had gone home and the boys were asleep. Michael and I, Rick and Colleen, and Ginny took turns the rest of the night, holding Karla's hand and snuggling with her in bed.

The next morning, Sunday, February 5, 2006, at 6:15 a.m., Karla took her last breath.

I sat on her bed, unable to move. Daylight streamed into her room. When Pastor Mike arrived to pray with us, I just stared at him and could barely speak. I'm not sure how long it was before I walked out and went into Brandon's room across the hall. I crawled into bed with him. I was afraid that he would wake up and walk into Karla's room and see his sister lifeless.

I was numb, but there were few tears. Brandon opened his eyes and asked me, "Mom, where's Karla?"

"She's gone, Brandon." I answered quietly. "Her body is in the room, but she's gone now." He didn't ask any more questions. We clung to each other as we listened to the people coming and going outside his door as they took Karla away. I found out later that Rick and Michael, together, carried her body downstairs; they didn't want the people from the mortuary to move her. I felt at peace knowing that the two men she loved most took care of her together until the end.

The rest of the day was a fog. I was tired and felt numb. Within an hour, visitors began streaming in: family members, friends and neighbors, members of Karla's dance team. Ginny stayed to help take care of the boys and the puppy. For most of the day my eyes were dry. Finally, I wrapped myself in Karla's favorite blanket and cried myself to sleep. When I woke up, the house was quiet, with just a few family members and friends still over, and the Super Bowl on the TV.

Chapter 26

And in the end it is not the years in your life
that count,
it's the life in your years.

— Abraham Lincoln

WHEN THE MORNING CAME, I didn't want to get out of bed. I felt empty and alone. I didn't want to live without Karla. But I knew I had to get up and begin planning my child's funeral — something no parent should ever have to do.

It was not the first time I had felt this pain; the year before Karla was born, I had a son born prematurely, just twenty-four weeks into my pregnancy. Rick and I named him Garrett, and he survived just thirteen days. We had a full funeral for him. For the past twenty years, his photo has never left my bedside. I still visit his grave every year.

But this was different.

Karla was both my daughter and my best friend, and our relationship had grown over years of love, pain, and joy — as did the hopes and dreams for tomorrow. As I lay in bed, tears streaming down my face, I asked God not only to get me through the next day, but also to show me how to live the next forty years without Karla. I cried and prayed until I found the strength to get out of bed. I walked into her room, knowing she wouldn't be there but desperately hoping to catch another glimpse of her. The room was still. Her bed had already been made. I sat down and looked at all her things, her pictures on the walls, the mementos given to her over the years, and I tried to feel her presence. I spoke to her, asking her to somehow help me get through this day and the days to follow. I knew I had to begin planning her service. Our first appointment of the day was at the funeral home.

I knew from the start that Karla's service would not be a funeral, it would be a "Celebration of Life." Rick, Michael, and I met that evening with our pastors, Mike and Scott, who would be performing the service. As we discussed our visions for the day, I imagined I was planning my only daughter's wedding day. That might sound strange, but I knew that the best way to honor Karla would be with a day of joy and celebration while also letting her go. I knew there would be sadness and tears, but I also wanted everyone, particularly her teenage friends, to gain strength from remembering Karla's smile and the hopeful attitude and spirit that she radiated.

Immediately, friends and family members stepped in to help with the arrangements. Clara, my friend from church who had organized meal deliveries a year earlier, arranged for friends to bring dishes to the service. Everyone's generosity was overwhelming. Those few days were a blur; I'm still not sure how everything got done. I knew that I wanted Karla buried in that beautiful bronze gown she loved but never got to wear to the Grammy Awards, which took place just three days after she died.

So, on February 10, 2006, nearly 3,000 friends, family members, and even total strangers who for one reason or another were touched by Karla's journey, came out to remember her. We had to hold the service at a nearby church, as ours could not accommodate the expected crowds.

Incredibly, the day of the service, my eyes stayed dry — even though there were tears everywhere. A friend has told me that, before we walked down the aisle behind the pallbearers, I placed my hand on the white casket and whispered, "Let's go, girl!" I grabbed my boys' hands in mine and, with my eyes fixed on the casket, we walked down the aisle of the packed church to Lifehouse's "You and Me."

We played a slide show of photos showing Karla, first as a baby, and through the last day of her life. In almost every photo, she beamed her radiant smile and was surrounded by the people she loved and who loved her.

February 10, 2006

I was blessed with the strength that day to stand on the stage, before the thousands in attendance, and smile while reading a eulogy I had written the night before. I spoke of the joys of being Karla's mom, as well as the challenges of raising a teenager. I spoke of her determination, her faith, her achievements in school and in sports, her generous nature and hopeful attitude. And then I said something that, a year ago, I would have been surprised to know was true:

This past year has truly been the best year of my life! We spent more hours laughing, hugging, kissing, sharing, and praying than some might ever get to have with their daughter. We did so much, thanks to our friends and family. The helicopter ride over LA was incredible! Feeling the love from so many — the cards, the letters, the flowers, the gifts, the meals — it was a blessing. We actually had fun going to the hospital. The doctors and nurses felt like our friends — they always spoiled Karla. Caring for her through this allowed me to have the ultimate mothering experience.

Michael and the boys were on the stage with me, and they, too, read touching tributes. One of Michael's passages especially touched me:

Karla's strength, determination, positive attitude, and love for God never failed. She was a true inspiration to me. She showed me how important friendships are. She taught me the true meaning of Amen. Her kindness and love for everyone was amazing and infectious. Most importantly, she taught me how to be a better father.

And Brandon, then just eight years old, wrote this on behalf of himself and Cole (with the help of their Uncle Tim), and read it at the service:

Dear Sissy,
You have been the best sister in the whole entire world. Thank you for always taking time out of your day to be there when we needed you. Your kindness always amazed us. You helped us with our homework and you would let us come into your room to hang out whenever we were bored. We will miss laughing at Napoleon Dynamite and eating popcorn while watching movies with you. You helped us to understand more about God and we will miss you reading to us. We promise to look after Mom and the rest of the family while you are gone. We love you very much.
Your little brothers,
Brandon and Cole

Then Rick and Colleen took the stage, and Rick spoke of how proud he was to have been Karla's dad.

Karla really helped pull me through some tough times. She was so smart and so mature for somebody her age. Karla was a beautiful girl, but she was a hundred times more beautiful on the inside. There is no doubt that God has bigger, better, and more important plans for Karla in Heaven.

Perhaps one of the most beautiful tributes was read by Carol Beener, Karla's sixth-grade teacher:

Karla was every teacher's dream; she was the model student. She was smart, worked hard, and was very well behaved. But the quality I remember most is how Karla conducted herself, and how she treated others. ... She was kind and compassionate, and she had a gift, a special gift, for help-ing to settle disputes among friends.
When I first learned that Karla had been diagnosed with inoperable brain cancer, I looked toward the heavens and

said, "What are you thinking? Do you not know that this girl is special? She's such a good girl, Lord, and she has so much potential to do so much good in her life, to accomplish incredible things!"

Well, over the last year, seeing all the lives Karla has changed, the positive impact she has had on each and every person she has come in contact with, and even many who've never met her, I realized that God had a perfect and wonderful plan for her life. And in typical Karla fashion, she took that plan and ran with it, gave unselfishly, and did it all with grace and wisdom that far surpassed her years. She changed more lives and positively touched more people in her short fifteen years than most of us will do in the fifty, sixty, or even eighty years that we may have on this Earth.

Karla's friend Adam spoke of how the night before Karla died, he and Melissa planned to visit after they got out of a movie. But they decided to wait, and visit instead on Sunday.

When I got the call on Sunday, the first thing I could think of was why didn't I go over there? ... I'm sure many of you spend a lot of time thinking of the things you could have done for Karla, but I know and Karla knows, and she wants us to think of all the things we could do and the things that we did do and can keep on doing.

After the service, many of the attendees headed over to our church for the reception. People ate and mingled, and the boys ran around, just being boys. I recall a friend coming up to me and asking how I was able to seem so at peace that day — he said it seemed as though I was the one comforting others, instead of them comforting me. I'm grateful that I was at peace that day.

Toward the end of the service, each person was given a blue helium balloon with "Amen" printed on it. Pastor Dave said a prayer, and when he was done, everyone shouted "Amen!" and simultaneously released their balloons into the bluest sky I had ever seen. At that moment, the sound system began playing the Beatles' *Let It Be.* I didn't see the boys, and panicked for a moment — they were still playing — but Michael took me in his arms and I realized that, at that moment, all I needed was him holding me as we, along with so many others, watched the sea of balloons merge slowly into the sky.

James "Bubba" Stewart and Ricky Carmichael in their
touching tribute to Karla, Rick, and our family

Chapter 27

I have let it be. But only because you told me that it was OK.

— Mary Lisa Emery, Karla's teammate

THE DAY AFTER KARLA'S SERVICE, Rick's motocross family invited us to join them for the San Diego Supercross. My first inclination was to turn down the invitation; we were all exhausted and in no mood to be among large, cheering crowds, but because his team had been so supportive over the last year, we decided to take the boys and go, along with my sister Ginny's family and some friends.

When we arrived, we noticed that all of the Team Kawasaki crewmembers were handing out blue stickers and wearing blue buttons. Then we noticed famed rider James "Bubba" Stewart had FOR KARLA across the backside of his pants, and the great Ricky Carmichael had the initials "GBRA" (God Bless Rick Asch) in the same place. Then, before the race began — with over 70,000 in attendance — the announcers asked for a moment of silence in Karla's honor. After winning his qualifying race, Ricky spoke at the podium about Karla's service and how her faith had inspired him. When James won the race, he dedicated the victory to Karla and her family. What a beautiful day, and how grateful I was that I hadn't missed it.

In the days that followed, I was caught off guard by the sheer number of people who approached me — in person and by phone, letter, and email — to recount their own stories of how Karla's journey had touched them. There were stories of inspiration, and how Karla's spirit had given them hope. People said they had become better parents because of her, and her friends shared how Karla's outlook had made them reevaluate how they took so much for granted. Though each story made me miss Karla a little more, I was also bursting with joy, knowing that my daughter had affected so many.

Not long after Karla passed away, the *Champion* published a letter to the editor written by Tom Bagnoli, a man we had never met:

> *'Why does she get to be in the newspaper and get all this attention?' asked my nine-year-old son Bryan. 'Lots of people get sick and die from cancer, don't they?' he continued, already knowing the answer. Bryan was making a reference to Karla Asch-Rosen. Karla being just another typical fifteen-year-old high school student. Or was she?*
> *I was first introduced to Karla's story by my wife Nancy. She*

had learned of Karla's struggles with an inoperable brain tumor through the Moms in Touch prayer group. Maybe it was the fact that I was a parent or maybe just because I was human with human emotions, but whatever the case, I was moved. We would pray for Karla and occasionally get updated on her condition via friends, the Champion, or the Inland Hills Church website. In December we heard how the tumor had miraculously shrunk. I remember feeling a sense of relief for Karla and her family. That night I held my sons a little tighter and thanked God. Life went on and so did I. Numb. That was all I felt the morning of February 4, reading the Champion's article on Karla. It stated that the tumor had returned to twice the size. What affected me even more were the words from Karla herself. She said she was 'really having a hard time' and 'I never knew it would be this hard.'

There was something about Karla's vivacious smile. Something about the heroic nature of her strength, the tenacity of her courage, and the depth of her faith. I began to pray and ask God for a miracle. The next day I became aware that Karla had died early Sunday morning. Tears flowed. How did this stranger, this young lady, affect me so? There was just something about her. Something special.

I answered my son the only way I knew how. I told him, yes, many people die from cancer, and no one person is more special than any other, but sometimes their story needs to be told. We were all looking for a miracle without realizing at the time that she was right in front of us. For a time, however long, however brief, we had an angel among us.

There were so many more letters that deeply touched my heart. Nancy, who worked at the beauty salon where Karla and I went, wrote that when Karla would come in to the salon,

...she would never complain or feel sorry for herself. She would tell me about being at the hospital and express her concern and empathy for the other kids there. Wow. Talk about teaching us all a lesson—no, many lessons. ... I will honor Karla by always trying to be a better person, a better mother, a better wife, a better friend... Everywhere and whenever I can make a difference—I will try my best. I will try not to sweat the small stuff, I will Let it Be.

Marianne, the reporter who helped share Karla's story with the community, wrote:

As a newspaper reporter for Chino Hills for the past 20 years, I have written dozens of stories about youth who are stricken with childhood diseases. The vast majority of families close the curtain in the final days and ask for privacy, leaving their stories untold.

Karla Asch-Rosen shared her journey—from beginning to end. When she was first diagnosed, her story stirred the entire community. Residents rallied around this beautiful teenager by sending her messages of support, holding fundraisers, and bearing gifts. Blue bracelets with the word 'Amen' were everywhere.

When her tumor shrank, her family boldly came forward to announce the joyful news, not afraid that disappointment might be around the next corner. That story inspired many more people who marveled that Karla was speaking to groups and reaching out to others. And finally, when Karla was in the final phase of her life, she didn't retreat into silence. She opened wide the doors. She proclaimed her story. Because of this willingness to open the curtain, Karla cemented a connection with the community in a way I have never seen before.

Dona, my friend and neighbor, wrote a touching note accompanied by this poem:

CAME THE DAWN

At twilight, rose the amber moon.
Stars through dusky night were strewn.
Quiet settled in the air;
The hush of slumber drawing near.
Softly, softly came the night
Of winter frost and pale starlight.
And quiet, quiet slept the town,
Awash in moonlight tumbled down.
And silent, silent slid the night
Toward the rising morning light.
As gently, gently came the day,
And mother's heart called out to pray.
Golden rays fell on the land,
Taking daughter by the hand,
Who rose to travel with the sun.
The dark of night at last was done.
The light, the peace, shone from above;
Sweet Karla freed with mother's love.

And then there were the letters from government leaders and politicians who had somehow heard about Karla's story as well. The San Bernardino County Board of Supervisors not only sent us a certificate honoring Karla, but also adjourned their February 14, 2006 meeting in her memory.

But again, it was the letters from children and teenagers that touched me most deeply:

...for some reason with karla's death i've felt a peace i've never known before. i admire karla for being our age and

being so full of strength faith and courage, and to be hon-
est i don't know how in the world she did and was still able
to smile through it all. i remember even in her hardest days
she'd come to school smiling, pushing forward, and that gave
me strength.
— Melanie

Letters and gestures like these brought me closer to understanding my purpose: to somehow keep alive Karla's spirit of
hope and inspiration. I just wasn't sure how to make it a reality.

Chapter 28

Every end is a new beginning.
— Anonymous

A MONTH AFTER KARLA PASSED AWAY, I met my friend Cheryl for a morning walk. I told her some of the stories I had heard, and how it seemed as though the entire community was sharing my pain. We began to discuss how I could best keep Karla's spirit alive in the community that had embraced her. I hadn't been ready to talk about this next chapter of my life, but as soon as the word "foundation" came up, the wheels started spinning. But whom would the foundation benefit? How could we make this a true community project?

That same evening, I discussed the idea with Michael, and the vision began to grow. I couldn't think of anything else. My first thoughts were to involve teenagers — especially Karla's friends who were in so much pain. How could we turn that pain into something constructive and allow them to feel better by making a difference in our community? Gradually, our mission started coming into focus.

When we considered names for the foundation, we considered Amen, the word Karla had chosen for the bracelets, but we didn't want people to think our foundation was connected to the church; though my faith played a large part in my reasons for starting the foundation (and continues to be my personal motivator), I didn't want anyone to think that one needed to belong to a particular faith — or any faith — to join our mission. We also wanted to avoid including Karla's name in the foundation's title. The foundation was not about Karla, but because of Karla.

The purpose of our nonprofit organization would be to support families in the Chino Valley who were caring for a child with a life-threatening medical condition. By helping with everyday living expenses, we hoped to relieve a little stress and provide some normalcy to their lives.

So, on June 29, 2006 — on what would have been Karla's sixteenth birthday, and just four months after her passing — we publicly launched The Let It Be Foundation, Inc. Our launch letter stated, in part:

> *Because of the desire to share the many blessings our family received during Karla's journey through cancer, I knew that letting her go wasn't the end. I can't have my sweet daughter back — but what I can do is listen to my heart and reveal both the blessings that we've received and the ones that continue to embrace our family. We know from firsthand experience what children and their families need during such horrible devastation — that it is the love, hope, and faith that bring a sense of normalcy. It is the peace that fills our days with joy; the peace that only comes from faith. It is the love that lets us know we're not alone and the knowledge that, no matter what happens, we always have hope in tomorrow.*

Grady O'Donnell, 8, making the first donation
to The Let It Be Foundation

The letter was signed by Michael and me as co-founders, and by the three members of our new board of directors.

Our first donation came from a friend of the family, eight-year-old Grady, for whom Karla sometimes baby-sat. He had told her one day that he wanted to donate his birthday money to help pay for her medical treatment. She said, "I can't take your money, but if you want to donate it to a charity, I'll help you find one."

Karla never got the chance, and Grady decided he wanted to be the first one to help our foundation make a difference. Now all donations received go toward helping families living with a child diagnosed with a life-threatening illness, just like our family once did.

Even at the beginning, we had great dreams and goals for our foundation, but at the time we weren't sure where they would take us. I did know, however, that the direction would come from what we had learned on our journey. Though our experiences were just a small portion of all that we needed to know, it was the perfect amount to get us started. Our inspiration would always be because of Karla, but our focus and purpose would be for others.

Learned Wisdom

Don't let the anticipation of pain prevent you from experiencing joy.

Chapter 29

When you walk to the edge of all the light
you have and take that first step into
the darkness of the unknown, you must
believe that one of two things will happen:
There will be something solid for you to stand upon,
or you will be taught how to fly.
— Patrick Overton, author of "Rebuilding
the Front Porch of America"

IT WASN'T UNTIL WE ACCEPTED our first families
into the foundation that we realized how much we had learned
from our own experience about how to help others in similar
circumstances.

We know that kids who are very sick just want to feel normal, and even if they know they may not be able to feel normal
in a physical sense, they want to do the things that normal kids
do: hang out with friends, go to the movies, go to school. Also,
they want the people around them to treat them as if they were
normal; they quickly tire of the sympathetic looks and the concerned "How are you?" questions.

We know that even families that consider themselves finan-
cially stable can quickly become overwhelmed as the expenses

Above: Me with my boys, Cole and Brandon, selling lemonade

Below: Some of our Junior Advisory team members, me, and Brandon (front) on our way to CHLA to read to oncology patients

related to medical treatment add up. Even with insurance, there are the unending co-pays and costs that aren't covered. The mailbox is suddenly filled with stacks of bills so thick they need to be rubber-banded together. Then there are the costs of frequent trips to the hospital, eating meals out, and baby-sitting for siblings who now have no one to pick them up after school. When a parent must stop working or reduce work hours to care for an ill child, it doesn't take long before a family is hanging on by a thread. Of course, some families are already living day-to-day when illness strikes.

We know that when a child gets sick, the whole family suffers. Siblings are left with feelings of sadness, despair, and often jealousy as they see the sick child receive so much attention.

We know that even a strong husband-wife bond can be ravaged by stress and financial worries when a child gets sick, and when the foundation of the family isn't stable, the rest of the family structure is weakened.

Despite all that we had learned, we also knew that we needed to listen to each family's needs and desires so that we could best tailor a plan to help them. Some needed help buying groceries, while others just needed a night out to recharge their batteries. We knew we didn't want to be a one-time wish-granting organization; there were already plenty of those. Instead, we wanted to be a source of ongoing support — not just for the sick child but also for the entire family.

It also didn't take us long to find out that our community was anxious to help. People volunteered their time, their expertise, and their financial resources. In fact, people from all walks of life called us to ask how they could help. They wanted to make a difference in their communities, and we were the channel. From housecleaning and lawn maintenance to paying for school supplies and dance classes, our continuing assistance has covered every imaginable need of the families we have cared for.

And then there were the children. The teenagers who knew Karla seemed to have the hardest time dealing with her passing. We saw so many signs of kids wanting to remember her — from getting "Amen" tattoos to putting RIP KARLA graffiti in the park. In the days, weeks, and months after Karla's passing, her MySpace page was filled with page upon page of comments from friends who just wanted to say goodbye or express how she had affected their lives. Just as I needed an outlet to help others while working through my grief, I knew that these kids did, too.

So, the foundation created a junior advisory board and hand-picked fifteen middle and high school students, many of whom were Karla's friends. The team raises money to provide room makeovers for the sick kids we're caring for. Every time I see the smile on the face of a child who has just seen his or her room makeover unveiled, I see Karla's smile when she first saw her new room, and I remember how her new room made all those months she spent in her bed more bearable.

As a foundation we have a simple mission and vision: gathering local businesses and people in our community to share their blessings with families in need by providing support and services. Today we are caring only for children and their families within the Chino Valley. Our hope is that someday The Let It Be Foundation will be in every community.

About a year after the launch of the foundation, an initial assessment meeting was scheduled with a family that had just been approved to receive the foundation's services. As part of our regular procedure, our family advocate (an advisory board member who is a healthcare professional) is joined by another board member to interview the family and determine their needs. I had decided early on that it would be best if I didn't attend these meetings, so that I wouldn't be confronted emotionally with more than I could handle, but this time, no other board members were available to go with our family advocate, Allison, so I volunteered. I was particularly nervous about the meeting because the child involved, a seven-year-old girl named Cheyenne, had been diagnosed with brainstem glioma, the same type of tumor Karla had.

The night before the meeting, I prayed that God would send in someone to take my place, but the next morning, no one called back to say they could cover it. I prayed while showering, and I prayed while I was getting ready. Then I went into Karla's room and sat there in her favorite green chair and cried for the strength to get through this.

I decided to bring Cheyenne something from Karla's room. But what would be meaningful to this little girl? And what possession of Karla's could I bear to let go of? I searched through her closet and drawers. As I was about to leave empty-handed, worried that I would be late for the meeting, I opened the drawer that held Karla's jewelry. There it was: a simple silver bracelet with an attached prayer box. Though I reminded myself that it was only a material possession, I was still unsure whether I would be able to part with it. I tucked it into the front pocket of my jeans and left.

I controlled my emotions during the meeting, though when I would make eye contact with Cheyenne's mother, her tear-filled eyes broke my heart. Allison and I tried our hardest to laugh with little Cheyenne; we even played games throughout our visit.

During the interview, we asked Cheyenne, "What is your favorite store to shop at?"

"I don't like to shop," she answered.

"Well, you must have a favorite store, don't you?" Allison continued.

"No, I don't," Cheyenne insisted. Then she caught herself: "Wait — there's a store at the mall that I like that sells only silver jewelry."

I had my answer to whether I should part with Karla's bracelet. When it was time to leave, I reached into my pocket and gave the prayer box and bracelet to Cheyenne. I could no longer hold back the tears of sadness, and — upon seeing Cheyenne's face — of joy. I apologized to her for the wave of emotion, explaining that the bracelet had belonged to my daughter Karla. As she accepted it, she answered, "That's okay, but I might start crying too."

And as she walked away with her mother, I saw her whisper a prayer into the box.

∽

Learned Wisdom

Draw upon your own life experiences, personal strengths, and talents to impact another person's journey

Chapter 30

It seems so simple appreciating life for what it is —
pleasure and pain, joy and sorrow.
For the moment, for today at least, I have learned to
be content.
— Gloria Gaither, artist and songwriter

AS I WRITE THIS, it's been four years since Karla passed away. So much has changed: Karla's dad, Rick, married his girl-friend Colleen. I know that would have made Karla very happy. Though Rick and I seldom talk, he and I will always share a spe-cial bond. Michael made a career move and was promoted to senior vice president, and I became a working mom — the foun-dation is no longer only a passion but my full-time job. Bran-don is now a sixth-grader, and Cole a third-grader; both of them dedicate many hours volunteering at the foundation, and serve as honorary members on the junior advisory teams. And Bent-ley, well, he's now a hundred-pound dog who rules the house.

I now see Karla's friends on a regular basis. For the first year after she died, it was seldom — but that was okay. Now, after four years, it gets easier for all of us, and each encounter seems as if a small piece of Karla is there, too. So much has changed for them: Courtney is in her second year of college and occasionally volunteers at the foundation. Nathalie is also in her second year of college; she has high hopes of being a doctor, and often visits Karla's grave. Melissa recently married Adam, which I know would have also made Karla happy. And Nikki is in remission and living her life to the fullest. She can be found volunteering regularly at the foundation office. We share a bond like no other. When my heart is aching I have Nikki to comfort me — she simply reminds me of my faith. And for her, she now lives her "new normal"; when she wonders "what if?" the cancer should ever return — I remind her that God's plan for her is here, not in Heaven with Karla, and soon the darkest thoughts turn into liberating laughter.

During these years, I've attended weddings and showers, participating in the joy but always aware that I will never plan or attend one for my own daughter. I hold on to the expectation that I will share these moments with my boys, which gives me the peace to get through these events, but as I attend them, smiling through my pain, I am always mindful that there are others there who are suffering, too: those who'll never have children, those going through divorce, those who have recently lost a parent, and those who are experiencing what I went through.

Every day without Karla is a challenge. But then there are birthdays and holidays when the memories come flooding back. In the weeks before our first Christmas without her, I poured my heart out in my journal:

Today my pain was so great I wanted to just cry all day. Somehow, the pain is bearable tonight. I have her room where her stuff, her scent remains. I want to close the door, trap her smell forever, but I can't. My boys need to play in there, sleep in her bed, and friends who want to go in there, I let them with pleasure.

Karla's MySpace page, once a place for her friends to write messages of support, became a place for them to share their grief after she passed away. Today, they still post comments directed to Karla, sharing funny stories they think she would have enjoyed, sending her wishes on her birthday, and telling her how much she still is missed.

Feb 1, 2010 3:56 p.m.
Some days i feel like its just too much and then i look down and this amazing blue bracelet i wear and remember you had the strength to fight and i realize i can make it.
E babie

Sep 16, 2009 11:59 a.m.
love i am writing my essay about you right now :)
erin

Jun 24, 2008 11:37 p.m.
A random lady knocked on my window of my car today in the vons [grocery store] parking lot and asked me about my loving memory sticker about you and i got to talk about you and how amazing you were and she was like tearing up in the end... just thought i'd let you know that you're still changing lives after you've left us girl. ...
Come visit me in my dreams soon please :)
MELtini

Feb 5, 2008 10:43 p.m.
these past two years I have never stopped missing you. not once.
not one day has passed that I haven't thought about you.
I love you and i still can't stand the fact that ur not here with us.
I hope all is well up there babe.
And for the rest of my life I'll keep missing you just the same.
Natty

Karla's friends gathered around her grave the day before
they graduated high school, June 2008.

One of the difficult milestones came for me in June 2008 — the
high school graduation of Karla's class.

A couple of weeks earlier, the principal asked if we'd like to
establish an annual scholarship in Karla's name. The first one
would be given at the scholarship ceremony. We were honored
to be asked. It was to be given to a young woman with an outstanding academic record as well as extracurricular participa-
tion that, preferably, included dance and/or soccer. The night of
the ceremony, as Michael, Brandon, and I sat in the audience,
I envisioned Karla on the stage receiving her own scholarship
award. For just a split second, she was there, and despite the pain
of that evening, I realized that if I had avoided the pain and not
attended, I would have missed that moment.

Just a week earlier, Courtney, who was senior class president,
asked me to help her write her graduation speech. She would be
on after all the graduates had received their diplomas.

The day before graduation, Karla's closest friends piled into my
Suburban. We bought smoothies and headed for the cemetery.
As the nine girls and I sat there remembering Karla, we reflected

on our memories. I made sure they all knew that I was count-
ing on them to keep me filled in on their lives' moments. Before
leaving, we sat in a circle and shared tender prayers. I gave each
of the girls a matching silver bracelet with an inscribed biblical
verse that was a favorite of Karla's.

As hard as it would be, I knew that I needed to honor Karla's
friends by being there with them on their special day. We attended
graduation as a family, blending in with the crowd at the top of
the bleachers. I tried not to dwell on the place in the program
where Karla's name would have appeared on the list of graduates. And as each of her friends' names was called, the sorrow
I felt over missing my daughter was overtaken by the great joy
I felt for them. For a moment, I imagined I heard Karla's name
called — only there were no cheers from family and friends.

When Courtney took the stage, I began to worry that her speech
wouldn't be heard and Karla would be forgotten. Courtney is
soft-spoken, and the crowd was already climbing down from the
bleachers and heading onto the field. The graduates' names had
been called, and all that was left was her speech and the turning
of the tassels. As Courtney began, it was difficult to hear her over
the crowd. But she managed to quiet them to hear this:

My high school memories have far exceeded my expecta-
tions… the fun, the friendships, the experiences, and of course
the football games. What none of us expected was to expe-
rience the pain of having to say goodbye to one of our class-
mates, who I know not only inspired me as her best friend
but also so many of you.
Today our friend Karla Asch-Rosen may not be here to receive
her diploma with us, but what she has done is gone before
us to display strength and courage. So, let every one of us
receive the gift of remembering that on the future challenges
too big to face alone — as Karla so perfectly put it — 'Just give
it to God and let it be.'

The crowd was silent as Courtney spoke of Karla. My heart was full, knowing that my baby was not forgotten. At the end of Courtney's speech came the amazing cheers of appreciation. It was a moment I'll never forget, how Courtney was willing to use her moment in the sun to make sure that Karla was remembered on this special day.

A couple of weeks later, on June 29, Karla would have turned eighteen. That morning, I woke up early and watched the sunrise. It's hard to imagine that my little girl would be an adult now, full of dreams for the future. There are no more dreams now, just memories of her childhood. The pain of having to live without my child is constant, but I get by because of the love of my family and friends.

I started a new tradition on Karla's eighteenth birthday. A few months earlier, I found, in Karla's wallet, a gift card to one of her favorite clothing stores, and I used the balance to get the boys a gift to celebrate their sissy's birthday. I hope this will help them remember their sister and her generosity.

As I watched many of Karla's friends head off to college that fall, I imagined what it would have been like, watching my daughter going off to face the world. I found solace, however, in knowing that Karla's memory played a part in some of her friends' college acceptances. Her friend Nicole dedicated her college essay to Karla. In it, she wrote:

Karla had a positive outlook on life that never faltered even when she was diagnosed with cancer. Anne Frank wrote, 'I don't think of all the misery, but of all the beauty that still remains.' This quote perfectly described Karla. She never let the pain of her treatment or the discouraging statistics of cancer take away her hope.

Chapter 31

*There are things that we don't want to happen
but have to accept,
things we don't want to know but have to learn,
and people we can't live without but have to let go.*
— Anonymous

ALMOST TWO YEARS AGO, I received a phone call from the head nurse who cared for Karla at CHLA. Barbara told me of a family from outside our local area who needed our foundation's help. Their four-year-old daughter had brainstem glioma — just like Karla — and the family would be moving from their home just as Hospice was coming in to care for her. Even though the foundation is currently set up to care for families only in our immediate area, I was determined to help this little girl and her family. It was hard to imagine how much worse our ordeal would have been if we had also been facing the prospect of losing our home.

Our board met and agreed that we could give a one-time donation even though this family was outside our boundaries. Our foundation does not donate cash, but we could give the family grocery gift cards to help them get by. When I called to find out where to mail the cards, I found that the family had already been forced to move and had left no forwarding address. I felt as though I had let down not only this family but also the CHLA nurse. It was an honor — and a turning point for me — that she now saw me not as a grieving parent but as a source of support for others. The worst part for me was living with the knowledge that I wasn't able to help this little girl and her family.

A couple of weeks later, my focus turned to my eighty-six-year-old mother. She had been diagnosed with colon cancer five years earlier, and each time she was admitted to the hospital, my sisters and I knew we might lose her. A few days into this latest stay, we were told she would be going home — but this time it would be with Hospice care. During her final eight days at home, our family was thankful for the tender, professional care given by the Hospice nurse. While it made me sorry that Karla had not received the same level of care, it also renewed my respect for the incredible service Hospice provides.

Days before my mother passed away, she told me that although she would miss us, she was looking forward to being reunited with my father — her husband of nearly fifty-seven years — who had passed away six years earlier. Like Karla, my mother wasn't afraid. That gave me great peace, and yet the heartache was still there.

My sisters and I were with Mom when she passed.

Before I even called Michael, I went outside to talk to God. I prayed and wept and even begged for a sign that my mom was okay. It wasn't that I lacked faith, but I was drained and seeking some solace. I waited, but there was nothing.

I went back inside to join everyone gathered around the kitchen table while the Hospice nurse, Lisa, made the routine calls. As I thanked her for the care she had given my mother, my sister Ginny prodded me to tell Lisa about the foundation. I gave her a brief summary of what we do, handed her my card, and told her to keep us in mind if she ever served a family that fit our criteria.

"I do know of a family," she responded, surprising me. "You might be able to help them."

Just then, it clicked.

"Is the four-year-old girl in that family suffering from brain-stem glioma?" I asked. "And was she being treated at CHLA?"

Lisa said she couldn't confirm it because of patient confidentiality, but she didn't have to; from the look on her face, I could tell that it was indeed the same family.

While some might see this as a coincidence — that my mom's Hospice nurse was also the nurse for the little girl I was trying to find — I knew that it was the sign from God that I was waiting for. It's moments like these that assure me I'm on the right path.

I asked Lisa to see if she could get me a forwarding address for the family so that we could help them with groceries. A few days later, she did, and it brought me great joy to provide a small measure of relief to this family in what was certainly one of their darkest hours.

I wish I could say that time is helping me heal, and that the pain of losing my child is subsiding, but the truth is, I still have moments of panic when I feel like I'm drowning and can't breathe. I still cry every day, but every day I also find joy. I try my best, as Karla taught me, to stay focused on all the blessings in my life. I'm so grateful that we had that last year together; I'm mindful that there are many families whose children are taken from them in an instant. I'm grateful for the love and support of my family, friends, and community. And I'm forever thankful that Karla's courage, her giving nature, and her sparkling beauty — both inside and out — influenced not just her family and friends but also the entire community and beyond. Because of Karla, I am now a better mom, I am now discovering my purpose, and I now know the difference between happiness and joy.

It's my duty — and honor — to keep Karla's spirit alive through my own life and in the work of the foundation, and to spread the message of hope, even in the face of adversity: "Give it to God and let it be."

Last year, on the morning of my forty-fourth birthday, I got into bed to snuggle with Cole, then eight. As he woke up, I said, "It's my birthday," and he responded, "I know." As we snuggled under the covers, he said, out of the blue, "If you could go to Heaven now, would you go?"

"You mean, if I could go right now?" I said, thinking carefully how I would answer.

"Yeah, right now. Would you go?"

Well, from the time Karla passed until now, I have openly said to more than one person that the pain was so great that I wished I could go to Heaven, even knowing I would leave everyone behind. But now, after truly considering my answer, much to my surprise, I said, "I know Karla is happy in Heaven and doesn't need me right now, but you and Brandon do, and I still have a lot of work to do here, so my answer would be no, I wouldn't go to Heaven right now." Without skipping a beat, Cole said, "Yeah, me either. 'Cause I still want to live my life."

And I said, "Me, too."

Cole, Michael, me, and Brandon, Fall 2008

Epilogue

SOMEONE CLOSE TO ME ONCE ASKED, "Why are you writing a book?" Initially, my intention was simply to share with others the story of how my daughter, Karla, had lived her life. Though Karla had left me with advice to offer about getting through a loved one's life-threatening diagnosis and how to pick up the pieces afterward, this was not my goal.

Instead, I've found a greater purpose. My wish is that this book will provide a message of hope and inspiration to those who are facing challenges in their lives: the person going through a divorce; the couple who discover they cannot have the child they so desperately want; the parents living with a troubled child they can't reach; the widow who longs to be with her soul mate. I want this book to give people confidence that they, too, can find purpose in their pain, and know that one day they will be happy again.

I know that it is hard for some to imagine or even believe, but I can honestly say that I have no anger toward God, then or now. I am filled with unanswered questions, so I continue to search and understand.

I have been asked if I would recommend not disclosing a diagnosis of a terminal disease to a child. Absolutely yes. I am not suggesting that we lie, but just as we talk to our children about sex or drugs, we also need to know when to protect them. If we are asked, however, it is our responsibility to answer honestly, and leave open the freedom to seek more answers. I believe that I did. Karla was an honor student with a laptop — if she wanted to know more, she knew how to find it.

After losing Karla, my time was consumed with the startup of The Let It Be Foundation — even as I cared for two very active young boys. I realize that I missed out on some precious time with them, but I believe that establishing the foundation is part of my life's purpose. It is a way for me to love and honor Karla while teaching my boys how to be better people and the importance of helping those in need. My hope is that when my boys experience their own heartaches — and like all of us, they will — that this book will remind them of how Karla never gave up. It will also show them how I survived and how they can get through pain — even when they can't see the light.

It has now been four years, and whether I want to or not, I am beginning the process of acceptance, knowing that I must live with a pain so deep that I can't reach it — and it is okay. Just as Karla so perfectly said, "The sooner you accept what's given to you the easier it will be." This is where I am. I know also that someday I must also learn to let go. I don't know how I will do this, but with God, my husband, my boys, my family, and my friends by my side, I will learn to let go.

As I write this I have yet to decorate my Christmas tree. The house is adorned with Christmas decorations as I force myself to celebrate another Christmas without Karla, but for some reason I have no desire to pick out a tree or decorate it. As for Michael and the boys, they don't seem to mind — though Michael does say after he buys a tree, "Are you going to decorate it?" My response, "Maybe, I'll try."

After a week of having a naked tree in the house, the doorbell rings. It's my friend Allison. She says, "I'm not asking you to help, but give me your lights. I can't stand it any longer." I laughed and hugged her. So this year our tree was lit especially brightly. Maybe next year will be the year that I do it myself.

Amen

About the Author

RUTHE ROSEN endured the unimaginable and then chose to turn her pain into purpose. One moment her active, vibrant fourteen-year-old daughter, Karla, was preparing for a dance competition; the next, she was in the hospital, where Ruthe and her family would learn that Karla had an inoperable brain tumor, and that even with treatment she was unlikely to live a year.

Ruthe never gave up on the possibility of a miracle, and it came — not in the way she'd hoped, but in a way that no one could have predicted. As Karla's illness progressed, so did her certainty that it was part of a plan much larger than her own future denied. It was as if something had taken hold of Karla's heart and mind, infusing her with a grace, dignity, and spiritual self-possession that not only enabled her to transcend fear, but also inspired courage in everyone around her. Despite her suffering, Karla remained focused on the outpouring of kindness and support from family, friends, community members, and the many strangers who reached out to help the remarkable girl who refused to be anything but grateful.

So began the journey that has defined Ruthe Rosen's crusade and transformed her daughter's legacy into a commitment to help others. The mission of The Let It Be Foundation is to provide support and services to families of children with life-threatening medical conditions, help them avoid centering their existence on a disease, and focus instead on the positives that can come out of it. The foundation has brought hope and comfort to families throughout Southern California, and is now expanding its presence nationwide.

Drawing upon the wisdom she acquired from living with Karla's illness, and the events that have led her to her current life's work, Ruthe Rosen shares her story with live audiences, offering insight, advice, and comfort. Ruthe is a woman of character and dignity whose kindness and generosity sets her apart. These, combined with her profound personal experience, make her a sought-after speaker who can help transform lives.

Ruthe's Keynote Series includes:

- Maintaining Normalcy During the Journey, Letting Go, and Moving on with Grace

- The Importance of Community Service and Outreach

- The Art of Compassion

- Additional appearances include keynote addresses to community groups on topics including *The Journey, Community Involvement,* and *Volunteerism.*

- Ruthe has also spoken at a variety of events sponsored by The Let It Be Foundation.

Media Experience

Ruthe has been interviewed, or has been the subject of feature stories in, *People* magazine, the *Orange County Register*, the *Chino Valley City News*, the *Chino Hills News*, the *Inland Valley Daily Bulletin*, and the *Champion* newspaper.

Her TV, radio, and online appearances include *Fox News*, *Fox Sports West*, NBC *Showcase Minnesota*, ABC News, KOCE (PBS), Time Warner Cable, LeSEA Broadcasting's *The Harvest Show*, 102.7-FM KIIS, 740-AM *KBRITE*, 1340-AM *WTRC News*, 95.5-FM KLOS *Community Spotlight*, KOST 103.5 FM *Sunday Journal*, and AOL *Good News Now*.

To email Ruthe Rosen about an interview or speaking appearance: **Ruthe@RutheRosen.com**

The Let It Be Foundation
PO Box 730
Chino Hills, CA 91709
Tel: 909 613-9161 / Fax: 909 627-6735

To learn more, visit **www.theletitbefoundation.org.**

For more information about *Never Give Up*, visit **www.RutheRosen.com** and **www.cypresshouse.com**

For book club discussion questions: **www.RutheRosen.com**

Resources

Family Support

www.ped-onc.org

www.faithslodge.org
For families of seriously ill children

www.supersibs.org
Dedicated to ensuring ongoing comfort, recognition, and support to children with brothers or sisters who have cancer. SuperSibs! helps these siblings redefine the cancer experience to use these life lessons for strength, courage, and hope as they move into the future.

www.siblingsupport.org
The Sibling Support Project is a national effort dedicated to the lifelong concerns of brothers and sisters of people who have special health, developmental, or mental health concerns.

Grief Support

www.comfortzonecamp.org
Comfort Zone Camp is the nation's largest bereavement camp. Comfort Zone Camps are offered free of charge to children ages 7–17 who have experienced the death of a parent, sibling, or primary caregiver. The camps are held year-round in California, Massachusetts, New Jersey, and Virginia. Comfort Zone

Camps create an environment where grieving children can have fun and break the isolation death often brings, while learning valuable coping skills for their daily lives.

www.missfoundation.org
The MISS Foundation is a nonprofit corporation committed to help families discover hope and eventually heal from the trauma of a child's death.

Saying Goodbye to Your Child
Ideas for a Special Goodbye

www.cancer.net/patient/Coping
Coping+With+Change+After+a+Loss

Relationships. *It is normal to experience changes in the way you relate to family and friends and in the way they relate to you.*

Routines. *When a loved one dies, the familiar routine abruptly ends. It is normal for family members to feel lost when someone close dies, and it takes time to develop a new routine that feels familiar and comfortable.*

www.hospicenet.org
If you are concerned about discussing death with your children, you're not alone. Many of us hesitate to talk about death, particularly with youngsters.

www.psalm23ministry.org
Research shows that religion plays a vital role in helping people cope with cancer, both mentally and physically. The psychological benefits of prayer include: reduction of stress and anxiety; promotion of a more positive outlook; and a strengthening of the will to live.

Hospice/Palliative Care

www.cancer.gov/cancertopics/coping
Palliative care is different from hospice care. Although hospice care has the same principles of comfort and support, palliative care is offered earlier in the disease process.

www.childrenshospice.org
Links to Resources
Southern California Support

Resources and Support Organizations

www.ped-onc.org

www.cancer.gov/cancertopics/coping/when-your-sibling-has-cancer
You've just learned that your brother or sister has cancer. You may feel a lot of emotions: numb, fear, loneliness, or anger. One thing is certain—you don't feel good. It's normal to feel scared. Some of your fears may be real; others may be based on things that won't happen, and some fears may lessen over time.

www.cancer.net/patient/Coping/Age-Specific+Information/ Cancer+in+Children/Camps+and+Retreats
Camps and retreats for families and children touched by cancer

www.sunshinekids.org
The Sunshine Kids Foundation aids quality of life for children with cancer by providing them with exciting, positive group activities so they may once again do what kids are supposed to do—have fun and celebrate life!

www.familyvillage.wisc.edu/general/wish-grant-orgs.html
Wish-granting organizations

www.bravekids.org
Helps children with chronic, life-threatening illnesses or disabilities by connecting them to medical information and resources such as financial assistance, camps, support groups, dental assistance, childcare, and health services.

Southern California Resources

www.theletitbefoundation.org
Mission: We provide support and services to families of children diagnosed with life-threatening medical conditions, and thereby restore a sense of normalcy in the home environment.

www.newhopegrief.org
New Hope Grief Support Community is committed to providing grief support through education and grief groups to all people of all ages who are suffering the loss of a loved one.

www.wecan.cc
We Can offers information and emotional support to families whose children have brain tumors.

Websites for Medical Updates

www.caringbridge.org/nonprofits
CaringBridge is a valuable resource for families facing cancer, premature birth, heart disease, or any serious medical situation. The personal and private CaringBridge website allows families to: journal about their treatment and recovery; ask for help with meals and transportation; express their spirituality; and receive love and support from family and friends.

www.mylifeline.org
A nonprofit organization that encourages cancer patients and caregivers to create free customized websites. A patient—or a

friend or family member—creates the site and invites guests to visit and participate in the online community.

www.patientadvocate.org
Mission: to provide effective mediation and arbitration services to patients to remove obstacles to healthcare, including medical debt crisis, insurance access issues, and employment issues for patients with chronic, debilitating, and life-threatening illnesses.

Young Adults

www.ulmanfund.org
We enhance lives by supporting, educating, and connecting young adults, and their loved ones, affected by cancer.

Additional Resources

www.marrow.org
Thousands of patients hope for a bone marrow donor who can make their life-saving transplant possible. They depend on people like you. You have the power to save a life. Take the first step today.

www.fertilehope.org
Fertile Hope is a national LIVESTRONG initiative dedicated to providing reproductive information, support, and hope to cancer patients and survivors whose medical treatments present the risk of infertility.

www.nowilaymedowntosleep.org
To introduce remembrance photography to parents suffering the loss of a baby with the gift of a professional portrait.